BEING
Bertha

HOW A WAYWARD WOMAN
BECAME A LOCAL LEGEND

Fran Genereux

 FriesenPress

Suite 300 - 990 Fort St
Victoria, BC, V8V 3K2
Canada

www.friesenpress.com

Copyright © 2017 by Fran Genereux
First Edition — 2017

Cover Image by Margaret Harris

All rights reserved.

No part of this publication may be reproduced in any form, or by any means, electronic or mechanical, including photocopying, recording, or any information browsing, storage, or retrieval system, without permission in writing from FriesenPress.

ISBN
978-1-5255-0251-4 (Hardcover)
978-1-5255-0252-1 (Paperback)
978-1-5255-0253-8 (eBook)

1. BIOGRAPHY & AUTOBIOGRAPHY, HISTORICAL

Distributed to the trade by The Ingram Book Company

TABLE OF CONTENTS

ix	**Preface:** The Talking Machine	85	**Chapter Twelve:** "This certainly is the life I love"
1	**Chapter One:** "always the best baby"	93	**Chapter Thirteen:** "Sure, I want to be with my relatives for a change"
7	**Chapter Two:** "a noisy crowd in the farm house"	103	**Chapter Fourteen:** "Make believe - even if you don't know"
13	**Chapter Three:** "Thank you, Papa"	117	**Chapter Fifteen:** "An unsettled life"
21	**Chapter Four:** Bring everyone together	127	**Chapter Sixteen:** "This is the truth, is it not?"
25	**Chapter Five:** The Homestead	133	**Chapter Seventeen:** "His Honour found the accused guilty"
33	**Chapter Six:** No need for an education	143	**Chapter Eighteen:** Prisoner #1590
47	**Chapter Six:** Together for Christmas	153	**Chapter Nineteen:** "Bear Paw Cabin"
51	**Chapter Seven:** "Galloping Tuberculosis"	177	**Chapter Twenty:** "It isn't what we want or like"
55	**Chapter Eight:** The Contract of Marriage	183	**Chapter Twenty-one:** Endings
61	**Chapter Nine:** "He's out for the evening"	191	**Acknowledgments**
71	**Chapter Ten:** "really living again ..."	192	**Notes**
77	**Chapter Eleven:** Wild West Show, 1920	194	**Bibliography**

For Bertha's family

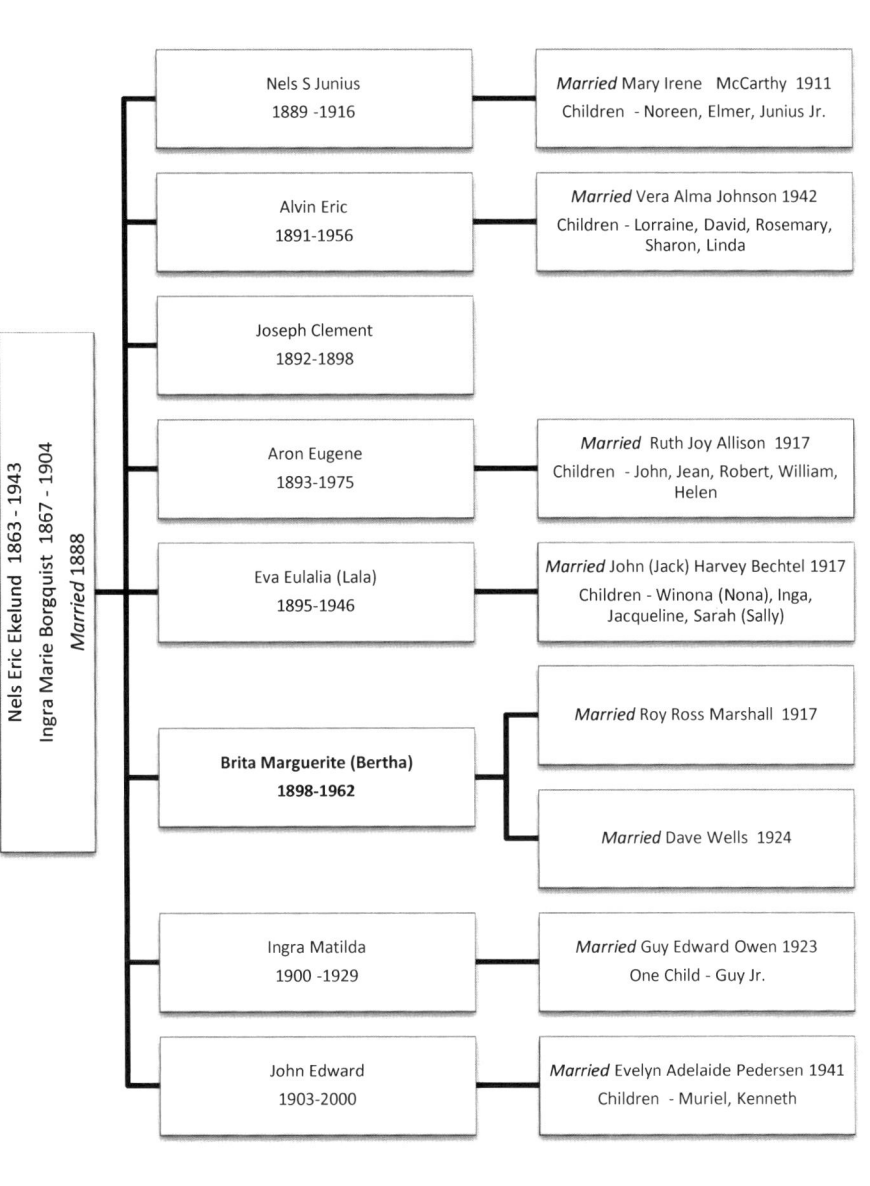

PREFACE:

The Talking Machine

Silent now, almost mute, the 1924 VV215 Victor Talking Machine sits in my home and taunts me. It is a sturdy piece of furniture that stands near the back door, a handy surface to collect keys and coins, purses and paper. It boasts simple yet classic lines that suggest a prestigious beginning, but now the rich mahogany finish has lost its luster and is marred by scratches, chips and dents. The thick green felt on the turntable is worn and greyed; the needle that swings down on the heavy arm is dull and scratches any record under its pressure. Records, thick and brittle, sit in the cabinet shelves, rarely spun as no one winds the crank on the side to bring it all to life. The Victrola shows its age, as it was new over ninety years ago.

But if we could travel back to the days when it was young, to the 1930's, when music and dancing kept spirits high in times of difficulty, it would have been the center of attention. Family and friends would have gathered around it to select the records of their favourite bands, to sing along and dance the night away. Lost are the stories of its journey from the factory and the names of its original owners. The early adventures of the Victrola are not to be shared. All that is known for sure is that it finally found its way into the hands of my great-aunt Bertha.

Bertha is our family's eccentric and our family's secret. Since childhood I have heard stories about her: stories of courage and determination; stories of creativity and abundant talent; stories of flamboyant celebrations; and stories, more difficult to hear, of abandoned children and deep depression. She was a woman of many hues; a free spirit, a trickster, a performer and an artist. But when I eagerly asked family members to elaborate on the stories, there would be silence, evasion and a quick change to a new conversation. I longed to know more about Bertha.

In the 1930's, Bertha's dream was to build and run an elegant hunting lodge at the base of Spread Eagle Mountain in southern Alberta. With the help of her family, she turned this vision into Bear Paw Cabin, a spacious, high-roofed log chalet. It was quite luxurious compared to the small homestead cabins of her neighbours.

The lodge was comfortable but the access was difficult. There was only a crude, narrow trail that climbed up into Blind Canyon, so it was a challenging task to bring in the essentials, let alone any luxuries. Bertha considered both a grand piano and the Victrola phonograph to be essentials. Both were carefully loaded onto wagons and taken to the cabin.

From its arrival at the cabin until the day that it was abandoned, the Victrola shared Bertha's life. For eighteen years (Bertha's most settled years) they knew one another intimately. If only the Victrola could tell me about the time they lived together. If only the Victrola could describe her daily moods, joys and worries. If only the Victrola could give me insight into the woman that she was. The Talking Machine knows the secrets that my family is reluctant or unable to share.

Bertha sold her dream home and left it along with most of the furniture for its future owners, one of whom was my father. When the Victrola was looking for a new home, I was quick to provide one. Once moved in, I gave it a careful examination and found a unique mark. From the front, my Victrola appeared to be intact. But when I inspected the back, I found a long cut from the bottom, straight up to the top. It is the cut of a saw; deliberate and destructive to the integrity of the piece. It begins in exactly the middle of the Victrola's bottom, between the two sets of legs. The cut extends almost through the top, where it abruptly stops.

I have learned that Bertha could be rash and impulsive. At some time it would seem she decided that the phonograph was too big for her space. I can almost see her on the day she removed everything from the drawers and doors, tipped the Victrola on its lid and proceeded to cut it in half. It is a careful and precise cut done with a sharp saw: she started at the back and cut three quarters of the way from the bottom to the lid, stopping to examine her work. She then moved to the front, thinking to match the cut. She was not trying to destroy the Victrola, just modify it. However, at this point in the job she realized that each half would only have two legs - neither piece, therefore, could stand on its own ... neither would be of any use. This realization only came to her after she had made a deep and damaging cut.

The Victrola is like Bertha. On first inspection it appears strong, whole, and in good working order. It will still produce music. Only when one takes a closer look does the damage reveal itself. It has a deep cut that came close to completely destroying it. I have learned that Bertha outwardly appeared strong, resilient and capable of taking on any challenge. She made her own rules. She brought excitement and a bit of danger to those around her. But I have also learned that she was often injured in life's battles. She had a stubborn, impulsive and incautious nature. Because she did not think things through and held little regard for the consequences of her actions, many of her cuts were self-inflicted. She bore deep scars from the loss of her mother, the loss of her sisters, the loss of her children, as well as the shame of a prison sentence and the ridicule of her neighbours.

I take another look at my silent Victrola. This time it causes me to smile. I see real value in this old friend and I would never part with it. It belonged to one of the most interesting and complicated members of my family. I did not know Bertha, but this phonograph experienced her touch as she wound it up; it produced music to make her dance, smile, laugh and perhaps cry; and it felt the bite of the saw as she modified it to fit her whim. It survived, and has prompted this story.

I have pieced together my interpretation of her remarkable life from those tantalizing family stories and anecdotes, as well as family records and the letters that she wrote to my grandmother, Lala. I hope you enjoy getting to know her, as I did.

Fran Genereux

Who was Bertha?

A lady, a lover, a liar, an imposter, and criminal -
  A daughter, a sister, a friend, a wife, and mother -
    All of these and so much more ...

Bertha's unconventional and unpredictable life spanned the sixty-four years between 1898 and 1962. She lived at the time of the birth and growth of Alberta and she left her name attached to several landmarks in Waterton Lakes National Park. Her story begins in innocence in Freemont, Wayne County, Utah, and ends with tragedy in Vancouver, British Columbia.

Bertha, circa 1920

CHAPTER ONE:

"always the best baby"

Bertha's family has its roots in Sweden. In the 1860's families in Sweden were large and good land was scarce. Recruiters from the Mormon Church promised that for those who joined the church and chose to move to the new colonies in America, there would be unlimited opportunities for rich, fertile land and a better life. Bertha's grandparents, Brita and Eric Ekelund joined the church and with their two sons, Peter Isak and Nels Eric (Bertha's father), left Ostersund, Sweden for the new world in 1869.

Bertha's mother, Ingra Marie Borgquist, also of Swedish heritage, was born in Utah. The Borgquist family had also been convinced by the Mormon Church missionaries that they would have a better life in America and left their homeland. They joined the journey across the vast American mid-west to the new communities in Utah. However, at some point, Sven Borgquist became disillusioned with the promises of the Mormon Church and spoke out strongly against the injustices he perceived. He left the church and joined the Methodist congregation, a minority group in Utah.

Nels and Ingra grew up in neighboring communities, and shared common experiences. After a conventional courtship, they were married on July 16th, 1888, in Richfield, Utah in the Mormon Church. They settled into life on a reasonably prosperous farm in Fremont, Wayne County. Their first son, Junius, was born within a year of their wedding, and the family grew quickly, adding Clement, Alvin, Aron and Lala in the next six years.

May 23rd, 1898 may not have been a remarkable day for world history, but it marked the beginning of a remarkable life with the birth of Brita Marguerite Ekelund, the sixth child of the Ekelund family. Her parents called her Bertha and welcomed her into their busy family life. Bertha's arrival was announced by healthy and determined cries. Her mother smiled as she held her in her arms.

Ingra kept a record of her children's development and wrote that Bertha was not a large baby, but "fat and solid". Her large, expressive blue eyes were remarkable from an early age. Baby Bertha caused her family little trouble; she was "always the best baby to be quiet with the lest [sic] attention her mama ever had". It was not long before she was walking and talking, always striving to keep up with her older siblings. Her happy but "sensitive and tender hearted" disposition made her easy to love. Bertha's first serious brush with illness happened when she was just two. She became sick with "hoopingcaugh", as her mother wrote it, describing her fear about her child's delicate condition. The toddler was very sick and took months to recover her strength.

However, even as a child Bertha's independent and determined nature was evident, and her mother was relieved to add that:

> *after recovering, she became stronger and quite independent; [she] would try to dress herself and*

wash and comb and sweep at the floor as though it was her duty to work at that age.

Childhood illnesses were not to be ignored, and the family often thought of the small grave in the Fremont cemetery where their second child, Clement, was buried. Clement had not survived an epidemic of scarlatine (scarlet fever) and croup just a few months before Bertha was born.

In September 1900, Bertha's younger sister Ingra Matilda was born. Only a few months later the older siblings came home from school with measles, which quickly spread through the family. Their mother struggled with five children all sick at the same time. This was Bertha's second brush with illness and her case was the most serious in the family. Her mother wrote that she "came near dying". Pneumonia and fever set in. The child was very weak and thin for six weeks "when she suddenly fleshed up and was never healthier before".

The Ekelunds were a happy, busy and hard-working family. Their farm included orchards and crops, a herd of sheep, a few cows and a sawmill. Nels was respected in the community as a carpenter and a blacksmith. Their year was busy with planting and harvesting, spring lambing and fall shearing, as well as community and church activities. The children were expected to do well in school and help out with the many family chores. Twelve years of marriage quickly slipped by for Nels and Ingra.

However, there was unrest in the Mormon communities of the early twentieth century. Residents in the area began to view Utah as over-crowded. There was talk within church communities that Canada was a place of promise, prosperity, and freedom from religious persecution. Thousands of Mormon families wanted to leave Utah to look for a home in this less populated area where the land was free and the laws were less restrictive. The United States had outlawed the Mormon practice of polygamy and some families were moving to escape arrest by US marshals. In the Ekelund family there would be only one wife. Ingra, refused to allow Nels to take another bride.

Although his family was prosperous and comfortable on their small farm, Nels had a restless nature that led him to investigate the stories of neighbours who were moving to Canada. He felt that he had been tied to one place too long and began to seriously consider moving his family north. He was drawn by the Canadian promises of free land and greater prosperity - new opportunities and adventure. He joined some friends on their move north and gained a firsthand look at the new communities. He liked what he saw.

Nels was a persuasive man and although Ingra was not excited about such a momentous change, he was not about to give up. He persisted. It took years of discussion, deliberation, and planning to convince his wife to make the move. But finally, in the spring of 1903 (their fifteenth year of marriage), when Bertha had just turned five, the family left Utah for good. They joined the growing Mormon communities just north of the Canada-USA border and just east of the Rocky Mountains. They left behind a warm climate, fruit trees and fertile land. They said goodbye to parents, uncles, aunts, grandparents and friends. With this move Ingra was separated from the support of her sisters and brother forever. Her reluctance to move was justified; she would never see them again.

When Nels left Utah he was filled with excitement and hope. Unfortunately, his life in Canada would prove to be filled with trouble and tragedy. He later admitted that it had not been a good decision. In less than two years, his family would disintegrate. Near the end of his days, he wrote in his life story:

> *In 1888 I married, built a good home and was happy. I farmed, had cattle and sheep, worked at sawmilling and was doing well. Then I got Canadian fever, sold out at Fremont which was the greatest mistake in my life.... and moved to Canada, another mistake. Here I have been experiencing in deep snow and cold weather for 20 years. Boy, my advice is if you have a house in a fair climate and making a living, don't move! Not north.*

The Ekelund Family, Utah, 1902
Front Row: Bertha, Lala and Ingra
Back Row: Alvin, Nels, June, Ingra and Aron

CHAPTER TWO:

"a noisy crowd in the farm house"

The family settled near the small village of Raymond on a farm a few miles from town. Perhaps at the time of the move Ingra knew that she was not healthy but put her worries aside, attributing the fatigue and pains to another pregnancy. The last Ekelund child, John, was born November 2nd, 1903, just months after they had settled into their new country and their new home. Ingra wrote to her sister and tried to describe life on the Alberta prairies with a family of seven children between the ages of four months and fourteen years. The children were immersed in the religion, music, and language of their Swedish heritage. It was a cold, winter night, but Ingra paints a very warm picture of family life in a letter to her younger sister:

At home on the prairie, 1904

Raymond Feb 9

My dear brother Sara:

If I ever!! I was thinking of John, pardon my mistake. I am so rattled when they are all calling mama. I'm hearing Aron read his lessons, June keeps asking what this spells, baby is playing with paper. I keep looking round to see that he doesn't get some in his mouth. Lala had taken Brita and Inga in the kitchen to play school while I write, they are singing so loud. Well lets see; now Lala is saying "turn to page 144 and we'll sing about my little dog. If you don't think Lala is a regular tom boy, yel and holler and run and play horse. She grows like a weed when dressed in overall (something she does quite often). She looks larger than Aron. Brita hasn't had a dress on for weeks. She does as much work again in pants as in dresses. Not so with Inga, she's always dressing up for some fine lady, calling herself Mrs. Brown. Mince and primp and makes several calls a day sayin: How do-do Mrs. Ekelund. I've just come from S.L.C. I's all well. I's got a baby to: I guess I'll go home to my children. It's time.

But of all the fun going it's the boys; they got pa to help them make a nice ox yoke and have yoked up two calves. They hawl water and go sleigh riding and today they went to Raymond to shop for me. Every business man on brodway was out to hale them. Crowds of kids followed them to ask questions, men stopped them to examine the yoke – they came home chuck full of pride and fun. They do look cute drawing the sleigh along like old work oxen.

It has been too cold to go from here to school the past two weeks so they have been trying the blacksmith and carpenter. They have tools. They have a nice shop to work in. We don't feel spring yet: cold, cold. I do hope we soon have weather the boys like to go to school and their teacher real well. Say sissie Iv looked and looked for that picture of yours you said you was having taken. Please don't slight me. I do want one.

O' I haven't told you how we spend our Sundays. After chores and breakfast over, girls hair combed all cleaned up, we all assemble in our front room – singing S.S. hymn from the mormon hymnbook. I read bible story comment on it. Junius read piece from S.S. paper uncle John sends also Alvin and Aron. We all sing hymn I play organ Lala and Brita and Inga recite pieces learned from S.S. paper all sing <u>amen</u>. The rest of the day is spent romping some like this. Boys dress in my cloth, girls in the boys cloths. Pa has some fool cap on, all dance to Pa's whistle and sing and end with a scuffle. Baby and I sit quietly and look on. I try to quiet them down again before going to bed and read a bible story while they undress to go. It looks lonely way out here on the prairie but I tell you there's a noisy crowd in the farm house. We all feel best at home this cold weather. I'd like to send you the rest of the <u>Alphabet</u> but I haven't got the inspiration to finish it yet. If I ever get inspiration I'll send it.

By the way do send me a swedish primer. I aught to send you some money to buy one but I only have Canadian money now and our stamps

> *can't be used in U.S.A. either. I'll get some U.S. money and send you. Tell me what one will cost. The children sing Tigare flickon these cold days. Alvin plays it on the violin. June does well on his guitar but he needs a teacher now.*

This is a happy portrait of the family their new home. This letter does not reveal the darkness that lay below. The move, the new baby, and the demands of her busy family had taken a toll on Ingra, and she described her concerns about an unexplained illness in another letter to her sister Sara. By spring her unsettled stomach and increasing pain had forced her to consult with her friend, the local doctor, Marietta Eaton Newcomb. Dr. Newcomb detected an inoperable stomach condition that she described as serious. There was no treatment and no cure. Ingra knew that she was gravely ill. Fearing that she may not have long to live, she started to plan for her family. She was consumed with worry about her children. How would Nels look after them? Who could best take care of them? Where was the best place for them to grow up? She wrote to her younger sister asking her to take her daughters and raise them back in Utah should she die. The letter was to provide written proof that this was her final wish.

In April 1904, her sister Sara wrote a distressed letter from Salt Lake City:

> *My dear sister –*
>
> *The letter you wrote made me sick. I did not know what to write in return.*

Of course if you should die and leave any of yours helpless you <u>know</u> I'd do all in my power, sister but it is out of the question - you're not. Make up your mind once and for all there is no one for them but <u>you</u>. Besides that letter would not do any good without the old man's signature in case of law. Of course if anything should happen it would kill me off to have anyone else care for them. Make your will to that effect and when I'm married and fortunate as you, I'll will them to you in the same way in case of the worst. My property if I have any --- "but wait a minute" you'd have to have the old man's signature ...

With love to all – Your sister
Sallie

The spring months crawled by and Ingra's illness worsened. Although she fought desperately through the pain and wished with all her heart that she could be there to see her children grow up, it was not to be. Ingra Marie Ekelund (née Borgquist) died July 10th, 1904, of probable stomach cancer in Raymond, Canada. Her life in Canada had lasted just over one year. She was thirty-eight years old and left behind seven children. Years earlier she had watched a scene that was now to be tragically repeated; in the year before she was married she had written to Nels about a neighbour:

Today Nels Anderson buried his wife. She leaves five small children to mourn her loss. What a sad sight to see that poor heartbroken man with his little flock, not knowing what to do nor where to turn for consolation. God pity them!!!

She could have been describing the scene of her own funeral sixteen years later.

Nels' wife, the cornerstone of his family, was gone, and he could not care for the children without help. All that remained of those Sunday afternoons together as a family was a shadowy memory. The Ekelund children would soon be scattered like leaves in the wind.

The decision about eight-month-old John had to be made quickly. Arrangements were made for him to be raised by good friends who had travelled to Canada from Utah with the Ekelunds. Anders and Ane Nilsson lived nearby in the small town of Stirling. They willingly took the baby into their home and into their family. The three older boys, June (fifteen), Alvin (thirteen) and Aron (only ten), were expected to stay and work on the farm with their father. Honoring Ingra's last wishes, the girls, Eulalia (Lala, nine), Bertha (six), and little Ingra (three), took the long train journey south to Utah to live with Aunt Sara and Uncle John (their mother's sister and brother). In three short years everyone in the Ekelund family had experienced great change, great loss, and great sorrow.

Little wonder Nels looked back on his move to Canada as a serious mistake.

CHAPTER THREE:

"Thank you, Papa"

The loss of their mother, the separation from their father and brothers, and the move back to Richfield, Utah, created very strong bonds among the three little girls. They clung to each other as they settled in to a new home with relatives who loved them but who were almost strangers. Each of the girls was affected in a different way: Lala, the oldest, shouldered most of the responsibility and became more serious and dependable, always watching out for her younger sisters; Bertha became more determined and more unpredictable; Inga, always the most sensitive, became more quiet and insecure.

It was a big task for Aunt Sara, twenty-eight, unmarried and by no means wealthy to take on these children, but she welcomed her nieces and lavished them with love, comfort and security. At the same time, her relationship with her brother-in-law, Nels, which had never been very positive, became more unpleasant. Sara blamed Nels for moving the family so far away. Now she was determined to follow her sister's last wishes, while worrying that Nels could change his mind at any time.

The return to Utah reconnected the girls with an extended family that included much-loved and loving aunts and uncles.

The sisters had only been in their new home a matter of months before the Christmas season arrived.

This Christmas celebration lay in sharp contrast to the previous year. In 1903, the whole family had been together, just settling into a new home in a new country, and experiencing their first prairie winter. A new baby was demanding their mother's attention. Getting established on a new farm was taking their father's time. With seven children, money and time were scarce and there could have been only a few small gifts for each child. Old friends and family had been left behind, leaving them to celebrate on their own. Ingra had worked hard to make it a special time, complete with traditional foods, songs, and customs, but there was an undercurrent of worry about her health.

In 1904 the girls had been transported to another new home and were very much missing their mother's presence. However, they were also surrounded by the love and attention of their aunts and uncles and the wider community. They were showered with treats and sweets and given gifts at every function they attended. There was peace and joy in their new home and great excitement Christmas morning to see what Santa Claus had left. Imagine three little girls with wide eyes and excited shouts discovering the surprises awaiting them under the Christmas tree. It was a day of feasting and sharing but at the end of the day Aunt Sara reminded them to send thank you messages to their father and brothers in Canada. The girls described that wonderful Christmas. They were quite overwhelmed.

Little Ingra was ecstatic!

> *Dear Papa;*
>
> *I got dolls and dolls. I got a little cup and some candy and apples on Keins X-mas tree. I got a little go-cart and a doll and a broom on our tree and a doll and a sack of candy on the Presbyterian tree and tonight I got a little dollie and a story book. My dolls are named Rose and Susie and Jill and Tiny and Jack. Jack's got his leg broke. They got candles on our X-mas tree. I love old Santa Clause.*
>
> *Merry Christmas xxxxxx oooo*
> *From I<u>ngra</u>*
> *Good night all of you*

Bertha excitedly described both giving and receiving gifts in a letter to one of her older brothers:

> *Dear brother – I've got five dolls. Norma is the biggest. She was on our X-mas tree. She's got long white curls and blue eyes and can go to sleep. I got Mary at the Presbyterian X-mas tree. I haven't got the others named. I got a little stove with two dishes on and grandma Mason made me a pair of mittens. We got candy and nuts and popcorn everywhere. I've had an entertainment down at the Methodist church and sang about the Star of Bethlehem. Lala was the Star of Bethlehem. I got my new shoes and*

the old ones fixed. I made aunt Sara a stocking bag and Uncle John a slipper case at school.

Lala wrote her own letter to her father and brothers on Christmas day.

Merry Xmas to all, (Happy New Year)

I got three dolls. Rachael Lucile is longer than my arm. She has black hair and blue eyes. She can go to sleep. Two little ones came tonight on the mail. I don't know what to name them. I got a lovely story book and a set of dishes, a lace handkerchief from grandma Mason, a pair of red gold gloves at the church and Aunt Sara made me a new green coat. We had a nice entertainment at the Methodist church. I guess the story book and little dolls came from Canada. Thank you papa. It snowed last night after we'd gone to bed. We had a happy day. We won't have school for two weeks. I'm glad so I can help Aunt Sara … we are all as well as we can be. We got up so early this morning I am getting sleepy. The Xmas tree was all lighted with candles. How is Johnnie?

Xxxxxxx Eulalia

When Lala wrote, "I guess the story book and little dolls came from Canada," she didn't intend to be dismissive of her father's gifts, but they were small in comparison to the lavish gifts from the family in Utah. Both Ingra and Bertha also mentioned the small dolls at the end of their letters. Nels had made an effort and remembered his girls at Christmas. He had sent gifts that he hoped they would like. Now his gifts were overshadowed by other gifts, and he realized that his influence was diminished in the eyes of his daughters. They were being raised in a Methodist community rather than his Mormon Church. He felt that he was losing his girls.

Aunt Sara and Uncle John loved those little girls and fully intended to keep them and raise them in Utah. But for Sara the expense was difficult to manage. She did not have the funds to provide for the girls as she believed was necessary. Though the relationship was strained, she needed to keep in contact with their father. About a year after the girls had arrived, Sara wrote:

> *They are doing fine here. They are doing splendid work at school, never have a sick day and when Canada is mentioned they only cry and beg me to let them stay. I've told them they'd have to go if you say so, and they like to see you well enough but not to go and stay. I've thought about it and think you'd better send me the money to keep them here. It won't cost any more here than there and then there is the R_R (railroad) fare for Eulalia. The money you sent paid for their store bill since July; shoes, hats, school [?] etc. They will need woolen underwear, wraps, goods for winter dresses, 1 pr blankets immediately. Please send the money ... Lala and Brita have each gained 7 lbs since school commenced. Inga is as fat and solid as can be. She grows like a weed. She wears 3 ½ sizes, a larger shoe but her boot is probably too small... I think it is your business to provide for*

> *your children. It is a great deal to get their sewing and washing and cooking done well and that keeps me busy. I can't get out and earn a living.*

Now this was costing Nels money. He questioned the need for all of the items listed. He questioned his decision to allow his girls to stay in Utah. With little warning and no discussion he decided to bring them back to Canada, and sent a letter to Sara about this change of mind. The relationship between Nels and Sara had never been comfortable and this letter increased the tension. Sara had missed her sister and family when they moved so far away, and raising the girls was her only way to do something for the sister she had lost. She recognized that she had her own reasons for wanting the girls to stay and tried to deal with these feelings in a formal letter to Nels:

> *Mr. N. E. Ekelund,*
> *Dear Brother in law:*
>
> *Your letter so completely stunned me that I have not had the courage to write you since. Of course I do not blame you for wanting your little girls; it is only human to become attached to them. I hope I am not considering them from a selfish point of view, nor considering my own feelings. I can only see that they are doing fine here…*

Sara knew that Ingra's wishes had been for the girls to live with her and that her real fear was that Nels would not respect her dying wishes. Sara wanted the best for the children, but also believed that their father was responsible to help with their upkeep. She asked Nels again to provide money for the girls.

Nels ignored Sara's requests. He ignored Ingra's final wishes. In his mind it would not only be easier but less expensive to have all of his children together. Within a few months he was on his way to Utah.

CHAPTER FOUR:

Bring everyone together

Nels had reviewed the situation. His wife was buried in the Raymond cemetery. His older sons, June, Alvin and Aron, were working with him in Alberta. His three girls, Lala, Bertha and Ingra, were all in Utah with his wife's sister and brother, and his baby was being raised by friends in Stirling. His aging parents were still in Utah but the arrangements made for his brother to care for them had fallen apart. Nels' solution to the disharmony and the increasing costs was to bring everyone together.

In 1906 he travelled to Richfield to collect his family. First he contacted his brother, and together they agreed that his parents, Eric and Betsey, would move to Canada. They were packed up and the railway tickets purchased.

The second step was to collect his daughters. He had warned Sara in his letter that he wanted to take the girls home. He arrived at her door with that purpose and pounded on the door. But it remained closed.

Sara had no intention of letting Nels take the girls. She wanted to honour her sister's wishes and protect the children from what she felt would be a much harder life. Her resistance was fierce and she refused to open the door. Voices were raised and angry words flew between Sara and Nels. The girls clung to Aunt Sara, who now represented safety.

Nels was determined to succeed, and he of course had the final victory. Anticipating trouble, Nels had arranged for two police officers to accompany him to Sara's house. When she continued to refuse to open the door, they simply broke it down. Nels tore the crying children from the arms of their aunt. He did not allow the girls to say goodbye or to gather any belongings. Their angry father pushed them out the door and into the waiting wagon. It was a scene of chaos always remembered by these three small girls: their father, in a rage, forcing them out the door, their aunt being taken away, in tears, into the custody of the police.

Sara was escorted to the town jail. She was charged with keeping the children illegally because they were not her own. She was forced to defend herself and her actions and was criticized by the elders of the Mormon Church for her behaviour. It required a considerable amount of time and effort to clear her name. She would never forgive Nels.

The tearful and confused family group boarded the train back to Canada. Nels was angry and determined; his parents were resigned but anxious about the move; the girls were devastated. They questioned their father. They could not understand why they had been taken so abruptly with no time to collect their favourite things, no time to say goodbye to anyone, and no time to prepare for the sudden change. They wondered if they had done something wrong. They wondered what would happen to Aunt Sara and Uncle John. They wondered what the future would bring.

The short two years that Lala, Bertha and Inga lived in Utah were perhaps the most stable, safe and secure they would ever experience. Aunt Sara loved them dearly and after they left she wrote to them often. They kept in touch over the many years, and the love they shared with her remained strong throughout their lives.

Back in Raymond, Alberta, Nels tried to pull everyone together. Baby Johnny remained with the Nilsson family, but the rest of the family was now in one place. Nels hired housekeepers to help his parents look after the younger children and prepare their meals. He took them all to the Church and had the girls brought forward for baptism. The baptism ritual in the Mormon Church requires total submersion and for this trio of confused girls it was one more frightening experience among the many.

They did not know who these church elders were, nor did they understand the meaning of the rituals. They were afraid of the men in long robes, and of the deep pool. Each child was led forward, helped up the steps, and forced into the water. Large, strong hands held them down as confusing words were spoken. It created another terrifying memory. Ingra cried, Bertha endured, and Lala resented being forced to participate. As members of the Church they were expected to attend the weekly Young People's Mutual (Sunday School) and to prepare to accept the possibility of becoming a wife to one of the elders - possibly a second or third wife. Lala, now eleven, was most offended, and once she understood these expectations, she refused to return to the youth group or the Mormon Church.

Nels had succeeded in bringing his family together in Raymond, and over time it might even have been possible to establish a stable life with the support of the community. But Nels was restless again and within the year he would force more dramatic changes on his family.

Siblings: oldest and youngest (June and Johnny)
Raymond Alberta, 1908

CHAPTER FIVE:

The Homestead

Nels decided to move his family again. He had a plan, and it was a particularly poor plan. He had explored the area west of Raymond and fallen in love with the spectacular beauty of the land where the mountains and the plains meet. The easy way to own this land was to take out a homestead. In 1907 he registered one homestead in the name of his parents, Eric Ekelund and Brita (Persson) Ekelund, and a second in the names of his two oldest sons, June and Alvin. The land was a long day's ride west of Raymond in a truly unsettled location.

The Homestead

Under the Dominion Lands Act, once Crown land had been surveyed and officially declared available for settlement, individuals could apply to homestead a quarter section (160 acres) of their choice. Then, after paying a $10 filing fee and 'proving up' their homestead claim (occupying the land for at least three years and performing certain improvements, including building a house

> *and barn, fencing, breaking and cropping a portion of the land), the homesteader could apply for patent (title) to the land.*
>
> *Dominion Lands Branch in Ottawa managed the homesteading process, although business was conducted at local land agency offices throughout the Province. When each quarter section was homesteaded for the first time it was given a file number and all documents relating to that quarter were placed on file until the land patent was granted.*[1]
>
> *Alberta Genealogical Society Index to Alberta Homestead Records 1870 to 1930*

Nels planned to work on his farm in Raymond and keep the family together in the winter. In the summer, Nels and his oldest boys, June and Alvin, would continue to farm near Raymond and he would move his four younger children and his parents to the homestead. This would meet the legal requirements of living on the land, establishing buildings and starting a crop. There was already a rough cabin for them to live in and a good stream nearby. He would visit and bring them supplies.

Even before the plan could be implemented signs of failure appeared. Eric Ekelund died in February of 1908, before Nels could move his parents and young children to the homestead. But Nels remained confident that he had developed a plan that was worth following and so his mother Brita, known as Betsey or Grandma, and the children were moved to the remote homestead in April. There they stayed until November. Nels intended to make regular visits to see how they were doing. This worked to some degree for the first year. Everyone was back in Raymond for the winter and then returned to the homestead the following spring. Nels was happy that this plan was working, but the rest of the family was less enthusiastic.

Bertha would look out the small window of their simple, rough cabin each morning to watch Grandma come slowly up the trail from the barn carrying the small milk pail. Bertha was more than happy to let Betsey take on the boring chore of milking their cow. She knew that early in the afternoon she would find Betsey asleep in her chair. At eighty-two, she usually had a long nap in the middle of the day. Bertha was also more than happy to leave it to Lala and Ingra to build the fire in the wood stove, make the morning porridge and the evening meal, and to look after all the indoor chores.

At sixteen, Aron was considered old enough to be in charge. Bertha would also watch him return to the cabin after he had been out hunting. He would carry the small .22 caliber rifle over one shoulder and often a rabbit and snare in the other hand. On those days they would have good meat for the stew. Bertha wished that she could hunt with Aron and avoid the confines of the cabin.

Often Bertha would head out to meet Aron. She might ask if he had seen any more tracks from the bear that prowled around the cabin, keeping an eye on them. After lunch she would often check the saskatoon bushes hoping there would be a good crop. Their food supply was always a concern and Lala was very careful about rationing what they had. Bertha was hungry. They all were hungry. And they were constantly worried how much longer it would be until their father returned with new supplies. Many times it would be over two weeks between visits, even though he would always promise to come back in a "few days".

Their homestead cabin was in a beautiful but remote location at the end of a rough road, about seventy miles from Raymond. There were no neighbours nearby. Often in the evening, the children would climb the small hill and look out hopefully to the east wondering, would it be tonight that they saw their father's silhouette on the horizon, coming their way? Would it be tonight that Nels would bring them food? Alone, the kids became a tough, independent and resourceful bunch. But they were lonely and hungry too much of the time.

Grandma Betsey was a stouthearted woman who had experienced her share of life's changes and challenges. She was born in Sweden and with her husband had joined the Mormon migration first to Utah and then to Canada. She had always worked hard and now, a widow at eighty-two, she was the only adult supporting the children at the remote homestead. On a clear August morning the young household gathered for their familiar bowl of oatmeal, but Grandma Betsey did not join the family. That morning their grandmother lay in her bed, unable to get up, unable to speak clearly, looking confused and worried.

During the night Betsey had suffered a stroke and was now paralyzed on one side. Although they tried to help her out of bed, they could not get her to a comfortable seated position. They carefully lay her back down and tried to arrange the blankets to keep her warm. She could only nod and give them a crooked smile.

The children were distressed and dismayed. They didn't know how to care for her. They didn't know if she was going to get better. Lala made a thin soup that they spoon-fed to her. They took turns sitting with her and keeping her as comfortable as possible. They watched over her night and day. They waited for their father to come.

One week and then another went by; Betsey showed little change and still Nels had not arrived. Bertha grew impatient and one evening announced, "I'll get Daddy". Her siblings were not overly surprised. They knew that their sister was often reckless, impulsive and impatient to take action. Far from being a delicate child, she was tough and strong. Bertha had earned her family nickname of "Tommy".

In the early hours of the next morning, Bertha saddled the one horse they had, packed a little food from their meager supply, and started on her long journey to Raymond. Her plan was to find their father, tell him what had happened and bring him back with her. She left her siblings with no way to go after her and now one more person to worry about.

The southern Alberta landscape is huge, with an unlimited sky and a horizon that seems to go on endlessly. Open meadows and gentle hills slowly swell as they approach the mountains. Rivers and creeks that flow in a manageable trickle in the summer months, are framed by steep coulee banks that require a careful crossing.

A rough wagon trail snaked its way across this vast landscape, linking the few homesteads and scattered post offices. Following the trail was not the shortest distance and Bertha decided to take shortcuts across the open range.

A good horse can travel seventy miles in a day - but it is a very long day - twelve to fifteen hours of travel time if the rider only makes a few short stops. Bertha was eleven years old and she made this solitary journey without hesitation. Independence, determination and courage were at the core of her personality, and they were combined with an impulsive nature and a frequent failure to consider the consequences of her decisions.

She was furious with her father for leaving them at the homestead, for "forgetting" to visit them, and for choosing to stay in Raymond. Her fury was her fuel for the journey. There must have been times in this endless day when she wondered if she would make it before it became dark. There must have been times when she wondered if predators were following her. She was alone in a big empty land, with her horse as her only companion. And always in the back of her mind were the nagging worries about her grandmother.

The day wore on and the sun travelled up the sky and then followed behind her as she continued her eastward journey. The closer the sun got to the western horizon, the fewer daylight hours remained. She could not afford to stop for anything more than a quick drink at a stream. Then she was back in the saddle to hurry along the trail. As she neared Raymond, she began to see more homes, better roads and a few other riders. The light began to fade as she rode into town. She knew she could stay with family friends. They might know where to find Nels and would certainly give her a bed for the night.

It was a very tired and gritty child that arrived in Raymond that night. Friends were surprised to see her but quickly fed her and put her to bed. Early the next morning she started her hunt and only when standing face to face with her father did she relax. She scolded him; she shouted at him; she insisted that he help them. Nels could not ignore the fury of his daughter. They started back to the homestead the next morning.

Nels took a few days to assess the situation and decided that it did not require changes to be made. He chose not to move Betsey from the homestead. He departed again, with the promise to return soon, leaving his mother in the care of his children. She lived just a short time longer, and during those days spoke to her grandchildren of the importance of courage and strength. She died on November 18th 1909 with the four children around her. It was Aron's task to make the second long ride to Raymond to get their father to retrieve Betsey's body and take it back to Raymond for burial beside her husband.

CHAPTER SIX:
No need for an education

Nels was not the only member of the family to fall in love with the dramatic beauty of the southwestern corner of Alberta. Both Alvin and June were young men now and ready to establish their own homes. June had a piece of land but didn't want to be a farmer. He was drawn to the mountains, to exploring the canyons and marking new trails. Alvin bought a small ranch a few miles from his father's homestead. He had plans to raise thoroughbred horses and build a great sheep ranch. With land he could take his first step.

As the older boys moved west and the girls grew older, Nels saw less need for them to return to Raymond for the winters and he left them to live at the homestead on a more permanent basis. He ignored these rough and tumble, ignorant and uneducated kids. It was Alvin who stepped in to take over where his father had left off. He confronted his dad insisting that these kids be registered in a local school or moved back to Raymond.

Nels was unconcerned. His attitude was that they had no need for an education. He was as usual preoccupied with ideas and schemes for mines and mills. To him the kids and their education were far less important. It was left up to Alvin to fix the problem. Alvin moved his siblings to his ranch and registered them at the Twin Butte School. The family called Alvin "Boss" for good reason.

It was not difficult to understand Alvin's motives. He was old enough to remember how their mother had insisted that her children get an education. She had been so proud of each of them when they started to learn their numbers and letters. She had encouraged them to learn Swedish as well as English. She had supervised their lessons at home and listened with delight when they could recite a poem or bible verse or when they showed any musical talent. She had praised their first attempts at writing and always encouraged them to work harder and learn more. He knew his mother would have wanted her children to go to school. This was something that he could do for her.

Alvin also had early memories of his maternal grandmother, Eva Christina Elf. She had been proud to explain that, before she moved to the United States, she'd been instrumental in changing the public education system in Sweden. In 1856, she was the first woman allowed to teach in a Swedish public school. During this "trial" she proved that women had the "ability, knowledge and character" required to be teachers, the result of which was a Royal Decree allowing women to teach in Sweden's classrooms. Eva's constant message to her children and grandchildren was that an education was essential for everyone. Alvin knew that he was following her wishes as well.

So Alvin arranged for his four younger siblings to attend the Twin Butte School. He knew that he was not going to school. He was almost twenty and would probably have been older than the teacher. Instead, he became a school trustee.

Horses and riders approached the schoolyard from many directions on the first day of classes in September 1912. Alvin rode with his siblings that morning, as he wanted to be sure that Aron, Lala, Bertha and Ingra were registered and placed in the appropriate grades. He also wanted to meet the new teacher. They rode into the yard through the open gate, past the solitary outhouse, and on to the sturdy barn where they tied their horses.

This school was typical of the schools that were being built in many southern Alberta communities in the early 1900's: a simple wood framed building with a coat of white paint on the outside. A small porch leaned against the south end covering the only door and protecting the entrance from the continuous west wind. Inside was one large room, with big windows on the east and west walls providing an abundance of natural light. Only on very cold, dark and wintery days would the kerosene lanterns that hung from ceiling hooks be lit. Hooks for coats and lunch pails lined the back wall.

In September the school needed no heat, but as the weather became colder the coal-burning heater that squatted near the back came to life. Students would discover that those close to it were often too hot, while those in the far corners would need an extra layer of clothing to keep warm. Near the back, perched on a small bench, was a water pail with a dipper for a drink at lunch. The classroom was filled with rows of wooden desks to seat up to twenty-five students, with a larger desk at the front for the teacher. The blackboard had the letters and numbers carefully written in chalk creating a border along the top edge. Above the blackboard hung a picture of the King of England. Angled in one corner at the front sat the piano. The few books that had been purchased were stored on wooden shelves along the side walls, and they would be carefully passed out for each lesson and just as carefully replaced at the end of the day.

When the teacher rang the hand bell the children gathered at the back of the room. There were twenty-three students in all, ranging in age from five to sixteen. Quickly they were grouped by grade. Eight children started grade one; four were placed in grade two. Ingra joined two others in grade three and Bertha joined two boys in grade five. Four older students including Lala and Aron were placed in grade seven. The younger students were seated near the front and the older ones in the higher grades distributed behind them. The wooden floorboards squeaked as the children moved to sit on the hard bench seats. Alvin smiled as he left, knowing that he had accomplished his goal.

When it was time to go to school, Bertha's emotions turned from anticipation to apprehension. It had been six years since she had been to school in Utah, and then it had only been for a short time. Since that time, her education had been intermittent and inconsistent. With the moves to more and more remote locations, her lessons had focused on survival rather than literacy. She wondered how she would measure up to the other children in her grade.

Bertha watched her siblings. She could see that Aron was reluctant; he was over sixteen and felt that he, like Alvin, was too old for school. He had been away from the classroom for too many years. He showed up for a few weeks, began to find reasons not to go, and was soon missing whole days. It was not long before he convinced Alvin that his time was better spent on the ranch than in the schoolhouse.

She saw Lala struggle as well. One of the oldest students in the school and grouped with students four years younger, Lala felt out of place. And when the school day was over, she was still responsible for hours of work, including outdoor chores, as well as cooking, cleaning, and washing. Her attendance was inconsistent. She fought her way through grade seven but early in grade eight Lala just stopped making the trip to school. She was seventeen years old when she saw the window for her education close.

Although Bertha could understand her siblings' difficulties, she was not going to let this opportunity slip away from her. From the first day of school she was energized by her studies and her fellow students. She never missed a day if she could help it. There were two boys in her grade, both more than a year younger than her and both full of mischief. They teased her and called her Breeda (she always hated the name Bertha and this was one more reason to wish her parents had called her something else … anything else). In spite of this, she loved school. It was a place where things happened, with new ideas and challenges and interesting people. Bertha was a quick learner and moved easily through her lessons. Often the older students would be asked to go over lessons with those in younger grades, and she took pride in her ability to teach the younger children. Given the opportunity, she was quick to answer questions, recite a text, or perform a song. She had a dramatic flair for speaking and writing that often inspired a smile or a chuckle from her classmates, and an occasional frown from her teacher.

A rural school teacher always had his or her hands full with the demands of caring for students across seven grades, of different ages and very different abilities and experiences. While the teacher was busy with other students, Bertha had time to work and time to play and time to think up mischievous plans.

One day she and some fellow students found a snake in the outside yard and brought it into the classroom. One of the boys gleefully chased anyone who seemed even the least bit frightened around the room with it, the teacher in hot pursuit, while Bertha watched innocently from the sidelines. Another day they placed a mouse inside a desk and savoured the screams when an innocent classmate reached in for a pencil.

Recess and noon were always spent outside. Lunches were brought in tin cans, usually Rogers Golden Syrup pails. The children ate quickly, sometimes swapping food or sharing it with others, and sometimes saving it to be fed to the dog on the way home if it was something that no one liked. Once outside, the play was unstructured and unsupervised. They played tag or Red River in spring and fall, and Fox and Geese in the winter. When there was new snow, there would be energetic snowball fights. Sometimes the students ignored the school bell if they were in the middle of an important game until the teacher threatened not to read the next chapter of the book they were enjoying if they did not come in immediately. And occasionally, there would be a real disagreement among the bigger boys that resulted in insults, threats and punches. The teacher would need to step in, break up the fight and get everyone back to their desks and back to work.

Most students had to travel several miles to school, so everyone arrived on horseback. There was a real variety of horses, from stubborn ponies to sturdy draft horses, dependable old plodders to young, partially broke colts. The Ekelund children may have been poor but they always had good horses. Alvin was a horse trader and managed to get them horses that were responsive and usually dependable. Many lessons about horses and riding were learned on the way to and from school, and all the Ekelund children became excellent riders. They loved the ride to school, meeting others along the way and often challenging each other to races and stunts. In the fall and spring it was exhilarating for them to feel the wind in their hair as they loped home. In winter it was a cold journey through the deep snow, bundled in as many layers as possible to provide protection from the biting cold wind. Occasionally Bertha and little Ingra would hitch up one of their horses to a small democrat buggy and drive to school like elegant ladies.

Twin Butte school students with teacher Mr. Brown
Bertha back row, second from the end on the left side, 1913

Over the years, teachers came and went. Sometimes a teacher lasted the nine or ten months of the school year, but often there would be several teachers throughout the year. Between 1915 and 1917 there were six different teachers at the Twin Butte School. It was a demanding job that paid fifty dollars a month and required one to board with a local family. Often the single young women who were the primary demographic for this position were courted by and eventually married to one of the local bachelors.

Bertha at age fourteen

Once married, a young woman was required to stop teaching. When that happened, sometimes with very little warning, a new teacher arrived and the children tested the new rules and expectations and then carried on with their lessons. There was little consistency in rural education in the early 1900's.

Three winters of school slipped by and Bertha grew from a twelve-year-old tomboy into an attractive young woman full of energy, curiosity and reckless courage.

From September to May the days were busy with school, homework, chores and routines. But the summer months were unstructured and the days were long.

Not far from Alvin's ranch and the old homestead, an isolated village was growing on the shores of Waterton Lakes. Named after a British naturalist, the park was first set aside as a protected area in 1895. Oil was discovered in the Cameron Valley and between 1902 and 1910 the village grew as a crew camp for the workers on the oil rigs. In 1908, Nels Ekelund discovered copper in the Red Rock Valley where he established a claim along what is now known as Coppermine Creek.

In 1910 lots were surveyed as the village expanded and visitors began to show an interest in the area. In 1911 the area was officially named Waterton Lakes National Park. The Hazzard Hotel and Livery Stable opened for business, a dancehall was built and a sightseeing boat made its initial voyage out on the upper lake.

The new park needed rangers too. Men were hired to blaze the trails, construct the cabins and build bridges. They were also needed to patrol the boundaries of this beautiful wild land. The oldest of the Ekelund children, June, was hired as one of its first park rangers. Now married, he moved his wife,

Irene, and his family to a small cabin at the mouth of Yarrow canyon on the park's northern boundary.[2]

Bertha found the summer months on the ranch to be boring and dull, so each summer she found ways to spend more time in the Waterton village. Her father was usually in the area, working on his copper mine claim and building log homes in the village. She used this connection to go to the park for an extended and unsupervised stay. The town was full of interesting people, mostly men. She got to know the early settlers and colourful local characters, the young rangers and the work crews. She loved exploring the area, and was always ready to go along for a ride or a climb. She was especially excited to realize that she was the first non-native woman to reach a summit or view a remote valley, stream or lake. She was always ready for the weekend dances and the parties that followed.

Bertha's summer education and extra-curricular activities were non-traditional and may have included entrepreneurship. The following article appeared in the *Lethbridge Herald* in 1989 pointing out how, in 1930, Mr. Wing Chow had been escorted to the park entrance and asked to never return because he had provided guests with more than good food at his restaurant. It was reported that, at the back of his building, guests could find drinking, gambling and girls.

Lethbridge Herald February 24, 1989

Waterton hospitality: Kilmorey, Wing Chow and Bertha

…Mr. Chow was not the first person to have operated a gambling joint, with sidelines, in the Waterton townsite. Probably one of the most interesting and storied locations in the townsite is near the campgrounds, Lots 8 and 9, Block 1. Here for many summers, starting before the First World War, a woman named Bertha — had a tent camp where she sold whiskey and beer, took a rake off from the gambling that went on and rented tents with or without the addition of a female occupant depending on the wishes and financial condition of the renter.

Bertha — received much better treatment than was meted out to Mr. Wing Chow … a mountain, a creek and a lake were all named in her honour… [3]

Frank Goble

Frank Goble does not provide us with the last name of this woman named Bertha. Is it possible that there were two women in the village with the same name at that time? Or was this entrepreneurial young woman Bertha Ekelund, a pretty and precocious teenager with a casual attitude toward men and sex? Bertha was a poor girl with a strong will and an impulsive attitude. She was free from parental supervision and guidance, and looking for approval and attention. Had she found a way to satisfy all of her needs?

There is documentation to prove that Bertha was noticed by one particular visitor during the summers of 1913 and 1914; Morrison Bridgland was a Dominion Lands Surveyor, a shy, quiet and conscientious man, dedicated to his work of exploring, photographing and mapping the Canadian Rockies. Most of his time was spent in the Jasper area where he climbed and named many of the mountains. However, he spent two summers doing a topographical survey of the southern part of the Crowsnest Forest reserve that included the Waterton area peaks.[4] The strong winds and unpredictable weather so common in southern Alberta hampered his work, and left him and his crew only able to climb and work about one out of every three days. He had time to meet the local residents and the local characters.

Part of Bridgland's legacy is the names he gave to hundreds of mountain peaks, rivers and valleys. It was Bridgland who named the peak that dominates the western skyline of the Waterton Village: Bertha Peak.

It was an easy next step for the young park rangers who were trying to impress her to lend Bertha's name to the small lake, the creek, and the waterfall that sit below the mountain. One local story suggests that the original name of the lake below Bertha Peak was Spirit Lake. But when Bertha Ekelund hiked up to that lake, she commented that she found no spirit there and that is was a silly name. Her companion, an enthusiastic young warden who was hoping to gain her favour, told her that he would rename it Bertha Lake just for her. It was unofficial, but it stuck, not just for the lake, but also for the stream and waterfalls that empty into Waterton Lake. Eventually a large bay on the upper Waterton Lake was added to the collection: Bertha Bay. No other name is used so frequently in the park.

Those summer days forever connected young Bertha to Waterton Park. Eighteen years later, a very controversial event would create an even stronger link.

CHAPTER SIX:

Together for Christmas

In October 1915 an envelope from the Alberta Department of Education arrived for Bertha. It contained her diploma, confirming that she had passed her grade eight exams. She was pleased, and quite proud, to be the first of her family to finish school. Alvin grinned when he saw the certificate. He knew he had done what his mother and grandmother would have wanted by making sure Bertha completed her education at the Twin Butte School.

Grade nine schooling was only available in Pincher Creek, twenty-five miles away. The students would board with families in town during the week and return home on weekends. Only a small number of rural students continued with their education because of the extra expenses of room and board. Bertha was more than excited at the prospect of continuing school and of moving out from under the reproachful eyes of Alvin and Lala. Somehow she and Alvin found a way to come up with the money.

During that winter she lived in Pincher Creek, attended the high school and enjoyed her freedom. The classes were interesting and she was a quick learner. The family she stayed with was good to her and encouraged her to develop her sewing skills, as she showed a natural talent and creative ability. This would be a skill that she would employ throughout her life, providing an outlet for her creativity and an opportunity for income. But what she enjoyed most was being unsupervised and independent. There were many young men coming and going from town and she was attracted to many of them. She easily fell into both academic and social circles.

Bertha's Grade Eight Diploma

It was during the weekends through the fall, with Christmas approaching, that family talk turned to the possibility of having a real family Christmas with all of the siblings together. They had finally achieved a sense of comfort and security and started thinking about the one brother who was still missing. Johnny, an infant when their mother died, had remained in Stirling with the Nilsson family over the past twelve years. As the holiday approached, the idea of inviting him to join them for Christmas took shape. The family could be together for the first time since that last Christmas so long ago when their mother was still alive. They decided to contact Johnny and see if he would come.

A few days before Christmas Alvin rode over to a neighbour's and phoned his youngest brother. "Would you like to come to the ranch and spend Christmas with us?" He didn't have to ask twice. Johnny agreed instantly. Bertha quickly saw the opportunity to escape from the next few days of cooking and cleaning that preceded Christmas. "Tommy" only helped out inside the house when she had no other choices. The trip to Stirling would be so much better than staying home and working with her sisters. She insisted that she should go with Alvin to get Johnny.

Early the next day Alvin and Bertha rode into Pincher Creek and left their horses at the local livery stable. The following day they took the train from Pincher Creek to Stirling, picked up Johnny, and caught another train back to Pincher Creek. It was a long day, and late when they arrived, so they stayed at the Arlington Hotel for the night, then decided to stay one more day and night after that. Bertha did some shopping to pick up the last few things needed for the Christmas meals, and to buy a few little gifts that might help to make peace with her sisters after their extended absence. Alvin made a few stops, including one at a neighbour's who broke and trained horses. It was a chance to do some horse trading and story swapping. A tall Texan, Roy Marshall, was working there, so Bertha didn't mind at all. She found this cowboy to be very interesting.

Finally, on Dec 23rd, they headed south. A warm Chinook wind was blowing and the temperature soared to 18 degrees Celsius. The three siblings rode the twenty-five miles in comfort and easy companionship. Arriving at the ranch, they were welcomed by Lala, Ingra and Aron. Oldest brother June, along with his wife Irene and their three small children, joined them for the Christmas day feast. Even Nels joined his children for the celebration. Johnny looked around at his father, his three sisters and his three brothers. He felt instantly at home and knew that this was where he belonged. That Christmas day they shared stories, problems and plans, looking hopefully toward the new year. The youngest son was welcomed home. No one could have predicted that the oldest would soon be gone.

CHAPTER SEVEN:

"Galloping Tuberculosis"

The family greeted the new year with optimism and hope. With the Christmas season over, life returned to the old routines. Everyone was happy with Johnny's decision to stay, and he and Ingra settled in to the winter term at the Twin Butte School. Bertha returned to Pincher Creek to continue her grade nine studies. Aron now had his own place and Nels lived with him off and on. Alvin and Lala worked on the ranch. June returned to his work in the park. The spring thaw, the longer days and the warm sun had the family expecting their best year yet.

June and his family had been an important part of that family Christmas. When the welcome days of spring emerged, accompanied by the usual abundance of wildflowers, the sisters decided it was time to visit their oldest brother and set off to spend the day with him and his family. They rode up to the small mountain cabin. Junes' wife Irene came to greet them, but the worried look on her face suggested alarming news. They were shocked to find that their strong and capable older brother had become weak and thin. He had little stamina, he suffered from fever and chills, and he had developed an incurable cough. It was not the visit they had expected.

As the summer months passed, the disease intensified. Frequent consultations and repeated attempts to help him recover had no effect. No treatment was available for what the doctor called "galloping tuberculosis". The family watched helplessly as June turned from a healthy adult into a helpless invalid.

June died on September 10th, 1916, and the family had to find a way to accept that he was gone, at the age of twenty-seven. In this time of crisis and sorrow, Nels collected the lumber and built the casket. Lala prepared the body. Alvin hitched his team to a solid wagon and, accompanied by Lala, took his brother on his last journey, to the Hillspring Cemetery. With only a few words spoken at the gravesite, June was laid to rest. Bertha did not go with them.

The shock of June's death rippled through the whole family. Without June to provide for them, Irene was forced to move with the children to Coalbanks, a town near the current city of Lethbridge. Alvin accepted the new role of oldest brother and continued to look out for his younger siblings. Lala fell into a deep despondency and struggled to find the energy to get up each day and face the hours ahead. When anyone tried to help she became angry and defensive. This was so unlike the dependable, predictable sister they had always relied upon that Alvin was worried. He was still in touch with the doctor who had helped them through their mother's death. Dr. Newcomb was now in Boston and Alvin wrote to her with his concerns. He wanted to find a way to help Lala through her grief and sadness.

Bertha had expected to return to Pincher Creek and continue her education, but June's death changed that as well.

Bertha was strong and she was needed on the ranch. She did not return to school.

Christmas came and went with the reminder of all that had been lost. Lala did not rebound. With the long dark months of January and February ahead, Alvin worried even more about her mental strength. When Dr. Newcomb suggested that Lala come and spend the rest of the winter with her, Alvin agreed and quickly bought the ticket. Early in 1917 Lala took the train east for a desperately needed respite from the family responsibility that she had never been able to escape. Her three-month stay in Boston was the perfect remedy. The time of relaxation and renewal gave her a chance to think about many things, even the possibility of registering as a nurse in Lethbridge. She was also thinking about a young man who was living in Vancouver.

A very bright spot in Lala's life over the past six months had been a chance meeting with a handsome young city boy. His name was Jack Bechtel. Raised in Vancouver but with dreams of becoming a cowboy, he had come to visit his Twin Butte relatives. He had come for a western experience but was secretly hoping to make Alberta his home. Lala and Jack met at the post office and Lala was instantly attracted to the good-looking young greenhorn. Jack had fallen in love with the country and the open spaces and soon also fell in love with this lovely young woman. It was Jack who drew Lala back home. He waited in Vancouver for news of her return. She waited in Boston for Alvin's ticket to bring her back.

Meanwhile, Bertha was busy on the ranch. But she was not happy. She was expected to step in for Lala and keep the household running, as well as help out with the outside chores. She was always bored with the routines of cooking, laundry, mending and cleaning. She loved to be outside but was usually given the jobs no else wanted. She hated it.

To make matters worse, she was now without her external conscience; Lala was not there to keep her from following her reckless impulses. There was only the Mormon Church school for moral guidance, and because she was suspicious of their motives she repeatedly failed to attend the classes. She had no desire to follow the strict rules of any church, especially one run by old men.

Bertha was hard to live with at the best of times, and this was definitely not the best of times. It was a long winter on the ranch. Bertha made her own rules. At eighteen, she was defiant and determined and would come and go as she pleased, returning only when she was ready. She spent time with people she found interesting and impulsively courted excitement.

In early May, Alvin was ready to wire the money for Lala's return ticket. Bertha knew that when her sister came back, things would change forever. She was pregnant, and when Lala returned, there would be no way of keeping her secret.

CHAPTER EIGHT:

The Contract of Marriage

Roy Marshall was a handsome, tall, lean, Texan with piercing blue eyes and an easy, charming personality. In 1900 the Marshall family had travelled by covered wagon from Coleman County, Texas to the Calgary area. The family included Roy, aged fourteen, his parents, his four brothers and one sister. Now, at the age of thirty, Roy was a seasoned cowboy with exceptional skill with horses. He worked a variety of jobs, staying put or moving on as he pleased.

Alvin had met Roy in Pincher Creek while Roy was working at the RCMP ranch training their remounts (replacement horses). Alvin liked the cowboy and invited him out to the Twin Butte ranch. Alvin was always interested in horse trading, and so was Roy.

At eighteen, Bertha was a petite, impulsive scamp who loved to manipulate men; she was a flirt and a tease. She was out to have a good time and enjoyed male attention. Her older brothers scolded her and let her know that they expected responsible behaviour from their sister. Her sisters discouraged her capricious behaviour, predicting that it would lead to trouble.

But between Roy and Bertha there was an irresistible attraction and a powerful chemistry. Bertha was headstrong, stubborn, and independent; Roy was charming, attentive, and drawn like a magnet to this unpredictable seductress. When they were together the tension in the air resembled the electricity that precedes a powerful thunderstorm. This was not a gentle and romantic relationship, but a competitive and combative connection that neither could resist. It did not take long for this romance to move beyond innocence.

Roy, Bertha and Aron, circa 1916

Sometimes Roy would arrive at the ranch and leave with Bertha at his side. Other times, Bertha simply disappeared, giving no reason, no destination and no return time. Inevitably her plan was to meet Roy. Sometimes she was gone for a few hours, other times she was gone for a week or more. Excuses were made for her obvious absences, but gossip was abundant.

What did the two families think of this? The Ekelund family did not see this as an acceptable relationship. They admired Roy's skill with horses and his independent spirit, but they remained unsure of his character. They knew that he was unsettled and a drifter. They hoped Bertha would lose interest as she had done with many other men who had courted her. They really hoped that eventually she would settle down respectably within the church and community. Bertha had her own plans.

Roy's family probably had less to say to their son; he was an adult and at an age to make his own decisions. From comments later revealed, Bertha did not have a positive relationship with the woman who would become her mother-in-law. Perhaps the Marshalls did not see this slip of a girl from a poor Mormon family as deserving of their son.

With Lala's imminent return and her secret pregnancy about to be discovered, Bertha took action. She left home to meet Roy in Medicine Hat and they were married on May 30, 1917, without her father's permission or her brother's blessing. Bertha had just turned nineteen; Roy was thirty-one. Expediency was more important than accuracy, as their marriage certificate shows:

The Marriage Certificate

> *These are to Certify that Roy Ross Marshall, Bachelor, of Cawly, Alberta and Breta Margrate Ekelund, Spinster of Carlslade Alberta being minded as it is said, to enter into the contract of Marriage, and being desirous of having the same duly solemnized, the said Roy Ross Marshall has made oath that he believes that there is no affinity, consanguinity, or any other lawful course or legal impediment to bar or hinder the solemnization of the said marriage.*
>
> *And these are therefore to Certify that the requirements in the respect of the Ordinance respecting Marriages have been complied with.*
>
> *Given under my hand at Edmonton, in the Province of Alberta this FIFTH day of MARCH AD 1917*
>
> *Issued at Medicine Hat in the Province of Alberta this 30th day of May A.D. 1917.*[5]

The young couple had little to start their life together, only passion and promises and an unrealistic idea of what married life would be. Initially Roy and Bertha were hopeful about their future. Their early relationship was romantic and exciting. Bertha saw it as a grand adventure, with only the small complication of a baby on the way. These two would spend the next forty years trying to work out a way to live and love together. There always remained the magnetic chemistry that drew them together despite their volatile relationship. Repeatedly they would reconcile, recognize their desire for each other and reunite with intensity and optimism. Repeatedly they found that this did not last. They struggled with their relationship until 1956, when Roy dropped Bertha at the emergency door of the Vancouver General Hospital and drove away, never to see her again.

Impulsive and reckless as was her way, Bertha had been the first of the family to the altar. But Roy and Bertha were not the only ones to step into married life in 1917. Older brother Aron had started courting a school teacher, Ruth Allison, and surprised the family with a wedding in July. Lala returned from Boston and Jack Bechtel was soon on his way to Twin Butte from Vancouver. Theirs was a swift courtship, and they were married in September.

The ranch was quiet now, with only Alvin and Johnny there to keep things going and Nels continuing to drift in and out of the picture.

CHAPTER NINE:

"He's out for the evening"

The young, newlywed Marshalls moved to Coaldale as Roy was working as a brakeman for the railway. June's widow, Irene ran a boarding house there and organized a room for them. She could use the extra help in exchange for providing them with an inexpensive place to live. Bertha hadn't really known what to expect as a married woman, but this wasn't it. She missed the ranch, her freedom and her independence. She hated the boarding house and the work she was expected to do. She and Irene could agree on nothing.

And it seemed that they were always short of money. Within a few months, Bertha noticed that Roy often came home on paydays without any money in his pockets. Perhaps there were holes in those pockets of his, but more likely a spell of unlucky gambling had taken care of the cash. The summer came and went and Bertha became more unsettled. "We must get away and find our own place," she complained to Roy. "I don't want to live in this town. I want to get back to the open spaces."

Roy realized that the conflict between the two women would soon erupt into an all-out war and that their current living situation was impossible. He contacted Guy Weadick, a friend who had a ranch in the Pekisko area just south of Calgary. Weadick needed someone to winter his stock; feed the horses and cattle, keep the water holes open and take care of the ranch. Bertha and Roy signed up. They could live in the rough, log cabin on the ranch.

Roy and Bertha, newlyweds, Pekisko, 1917

This little building had two cramped rooms and two small windows that were stingy with the light they let in. The ceiling was low and Roy had to stoop to enter through the low, narrow door. Inside there was a wood stove for heat and a rough counter along the wall by the door with a spot for the water bucket to sit after it had been filled at the well. The back bedroom was dark and cold by morning. None of this worried Bertha; she had experienced hardship before and this was better than living in another woman's house. Roy was less enthusiastic and less optimistic. He preferred a comfortable warm house, good food on the table, and opportunities to spend time talking with friends, old and new.

The couple had little to take with them for the move. They made the cabin as comfortable as possible by scrounging furniture and making sure they found good warm blankets; they brought in basic provisions for the winter months ahead; they cut wood to see them through the cold days to come; they made sure they had a good water source and carried water to the cabin for daily use.

There were no comforts here. Bertha thought the isolated little cabin would be a prefect, romantic nest. But the winter of 1917-1918 turned out to be cold and cruel.

As they set about the steady daily work of wintering cattle and horses, Bertha found challenges and kept busy. She noticed beavers in the nearby lake so she set some traps and caught and skinned the animals and then tanned the hides. She prized these pelts and proudly showed them off in the years to come as part of a stylish urban wardrobe.

Bertha wouldn't let her pregnancy slow her down. She refused to let it stop her from doing her share of the work. Although she had felt sick and irritable for the first few months and been unusually hard to deal with, as the pregnancy advanced she regained her energy and some of her positive outlook.

But Bertha's moods, always unpredictable, could change as quickly as the Alberta weather. She had mixed feelings about the pregnancy. She began to realize that this was not the exciting future she had dreamed of. She had envisioned a life of grand adventure, and now she was a wife and soon-to-be mother. Because her mother had died when she was very young, and no one had filled the gap, she was unsure of how she would fare as a mother. There were times when she felt trapped and did not want the baby, but there were also times when she realized that a small miracle was happening inside her, and she was excited because she would have someone to love and there would be someone to love her in return.

The cabin was small. The nights were long and dark. There was little variety in the daily tasks of feeding the cattle, checking the horses, opening the water holes and keeping the cabin warm. The Marshalls had few visitors and the routine began to create stress in the love nest. They were two restless people in a space that was too small, for too long. Something had to give. Roy started to look for reasons to get away. He visited the neighbours. He rode out for provisions. His visits to see his mother in Calgary became more frequent, and one day he told Bertha that he would be away for a few days. Resentment grew as she watched Roy saddle his horse and ride out of the yard.

She felt angry and abandoned. In December, the days are short and the weather unforgiving. Bertha was alone and her moods were dark. She saddled her horse to check the cows and put out some feed. The snow was deep and she realized that she was not going to be able to get the job done alone. She rode over to a neighbour's house where there was a phone and called the Marshall house in Calgary. The call was picked up by Mrs. Marshall, senior. When Bertha told her that she needed Roy to come home and help her with the work, she was told: "Roy's not in. He is out for the evening with his school teacher friend. I'll tell him you called." No help was coming.

Now Bertha was furious and became reckless. She started home at a quick pace. She was careless as she pushed her horse too fast through the snow and patches of ice. The mare stumbled in a drift and went down with her rider. It was a hard impact and Bertha felt that something inside changed. There was a different and unexpected pain.

The mare stood up and Bertha pulled herself back into to the saddle and carefully found her way back to the small log cabin. The discomfort increased and although she wasn't sure what would happen next, she was sure she could manage.

As the day turned into evening, the pain intensified and she realized that she had gone into labour. She knew she needed help, but it was too late to go out again. The baby was coming. It was cold. It was dark. Alone, she prepared for the birth of her child.

Growing up with animals, Bertha had seen many births – colts, lambs and calves - and knew what animals experienced. This, however, seemed very different. She thought she knew what was going to happen, but the intensity of the labour pains caught her by surprise. The pain came in waves. She screamed, she cried, and she cursed Roy.

The hours crawled by. Alone in the small, dark, cold cabin Bertha delivered her baby girl. The baby was not strong; her cry was weak. Bertha cut the umbilical cord and delivered the afterbirth. She held the small girl close, caressed her tiny hands, and kissed her damp forehead. It was only a few hours before the tiny heart stopped beating, but Bertha continued to hold the unmoving child in her arms, tears streaming down her face.

In Calgary, Roy came in late from his evening out and headed to bed. It was only in the morning that his mother gave him the message that Bertha had called and wanted him to come home. He sensed that she would not have called unless she was really angry with him, or because something was wrong. He wasted no time getting on his horse and starting the ride to Pekisko.

It was far too late when Roy arrived. When he entered the cabin, he found a grim scene: the rooms were dark and cold, as the fire had gone out hours ago. From the disorder around him, he knew that Bertha had done everything she could to survive a terrible night. In the back room, wrapped in coats and blankets, he found his wife and their baby. He would never forget the look on her face – an expression that combined absolute hate and absolute love. He didn't know how to ask to be forgiven as he gently pulled the infant from her arms.

Bertha was exhausted and Roy sensed that she needed a doctor's help. He quickly built up the fire to warm the cabin. He tenderly placed Bertha on the bed and wrapped her in the quilts he could find. She remained pale and silent. She would not talk to him. It seemed that something had broken within her.

The nearest doctor was in High River, almost thirty miles away. With the promise of the quickest possible return, Roy left his wife again. He rode like a man possessed, like the devil himself, giving his horse no rest over the entire frantic journey. It was a desperate man who finally found the doctor and insisted he come back to the Pekisko ranch.

They found Bertha still in bed. She had not moved. She permitted an examination. She listened quietly to the doctor's instructions. She agreed to do what she was told.

Physically, Bertha would recover, but she needed time to regain her strength. Roy tried to make up for being away. He promised he would stay close. He took over all the work and let her have time to herself.

Emotionally, Bertha had experienced unforgettable pain that she would carry forever. She would never look at her husband in the same way again. She had watched her baby die and been close to death herself. The depression that waited in the background for so many members of her family moved in on her. She would not, or could not, be consoled. The worst of the winter still loomed ahead of them.

As her twentieth birthday approached in May, Bertha considered what life had given her: an abundance of loss and abandonment all tied up in painful memories. She remembered her loving mother who died when she was just six years old, and who was now just a shadow in her memory. She remembered her short time with her Aunt Sara. Those were happy days until her father had arrived and literally pulled the three girls from the arms of their aunt and packaged them back to Canada. She remembered her Grandma Betsey, who had lived with them at the homestead, and she remembered how Betsey had suffered and died slowly. These were the women who could have led her into adulthood, who could have provided the life lessons she needed. But she had been denied their guidance and love. And in this cruel winter she had watched her innocent baby girl die in her arms. She was a daughter who had lost her mother, and now a mother who had lost her daughter. Females, she believed, were not there when you needed them.

Bertha's perception of men was also distorted. Her father was unpredictable and unreliable, and had little time for his daughters. He had allowed the family to be scattered, and later abandoned them at the Waterton homestead … who even knew for sure where he was now? Her brothers were at times helpful and supportive, but at times critical, bossy and demanding. They were busy getting on with their own lives and dealing with their own problems, and often they only saw her as one of those problems. Now the man she had impulsively chosen as her husband had proven himself to be dishonest and hurtful. Men, she believed, were not to be trusted.

During the long winter months in Pekisko Bertha's worldview shifted. She realized that she was strong, determined and brave, but that she could also be overcome by terrible depression. She did her best to draw on her inner strength and move forward. As she worked her way through the confusion and grief that followed her daughter's death, she decided that the world was an uncaring place and so, in response, she could be an uncaring person. She promised never again to find herself in such a vulnerable position. She would make her own decisions; she would live by her own rules; she would guard her independence. She built layers of emotional armour around her as protection from being hurt so deeply again.

With spring came the warming sun, the longer days, and the melting snow. Hopeful crocuses bloomed on the hillsides, shoots of green appeared in the dead brown grass, and a gradual thaw began to soften Bertha's grief. Staying at the Pekisko ranch was unthinkable. Her marriage was damaged beyond repair. Roy headed in one direction, and Bertha went another—'home' to Alvin's ranch in Twin Butte.

So much had changed in the twelve months since she had run away to marry Roy. Aron and Ruth had moved on. Lala was happily married to Jack and they were establishing their own place. Ingra had gone off to Lethbridge to secretarial school. June's death was still an unhealed wound and she would have nothing to do with his widow. Only Alvin and Johnny were left at the ranch. There was only one thing that hadn't changed - Nels was as restless as ever and still searching for his future fortune.

She moved back into Alvin's house. She spent time with Lala. She planned and re-planned places to go with Ingra. She visited family and friends. For six months she searched for a way forward, knowing what she really needed was a fresh start.

CHAPTER TEN:
"really living again ..."

Bertha decided to create a clean slate and erase all evidence of her previous impulsive and improper behaviors. She wanted to go to a place where no one knew her or her reputation. She planned a getaway, and in November of 1918 she boarded the train to Portland, Oregon, claiming in her usual dramatic fashion that she was leaving "for good".

Bertha gave no reason for choosing Portland. Trying to understand Bertha was - and still is - like trying to catch a sheet of paper caught by the wind: it's gone from you just as you think you have it.

She chose a city with snow-capped mountains and ocean beaches. By this time, Ingra had finished her schooling and was excited to join Bertha on her new adventure. They arrived in a busy, growing city, just weeks after the November 11th headlines shouted "Armistice Signed - End of the War!"

World War One was over. Peace was promised. The city atmosphere was optimistic and vibrant, and everywhere the sense of a new beginning reinforced Bertha's decision. For several years, women had been encouraged to become part of the workforce as the men had gone to fight. And although the soldiers would soon be returning and looking for work, there were jobs to be had. Bertha and Ingra were capable smart women. They soon found employment at the Benson Hotel telephone switchboard. They settled in Portland for the winter months and enjoyed their new and exciting lifestyle.

How different the world for the three sisters at this time! And how different their perspectives on life! Lala, dependable, serious, responsible, married to a reliable and conscientious man, was now pregnant after a respectable fourteen months. Although she was living in an old homesteader's cabin that shook when the wind blew, she could see a promising future and was planning and working to build a ranch and a home that would be safe and secure. Bertha unpredictable, impulsive, careless, was on her own after a hasty marriage to an unfaithful gambler, scarred by her baby girl's death. She had wrapped herself in a protective shield and was living for the moment enjoying interesting new ventures, with no one to care about but herself. And Ingra, naïve and hopeful, was living in the shadow of her outgoing

Ingra and Bertha Portland, 1919

older sister, expecting that she would have a long life of happiness and prosperity.

In spite of the attractiveness of this life in Portland, the ties to home were strong, and with spring approaching the girls were pulled back to Alberta. Ingra was there in May, and Bertha showed up in July. "For good" turned out to be about eight months. The arrival of Lala's first baby girl, Nona, may have been the deciding factor. Perhaps the sisters had planned a short visit, but they ended up staying for several months.

The summer of 1919 was very hot and very dry. Everyone watched the Alberta sky for clouds and hoped for rain. They were teased on many days when huge white thunderheads built up in the west, rumbled with thunder and flashed with lightning, but produced no rain. They were tested by destructive hailstorms that stripped the leaves off the plants and trees but left no real moisture.

The crops wilted in the fields and there was no hay to put up for winter feed for the livestock. Fires started in the dry trees and the air was at times thick with smoke. The summer wore on and the drought became more severe. Neighbours throughout the community reluctantly sold their cattle and horses. Bertha helped out where she could. She worked with Alvin in the fields pulling brush. She joined her sisters when they rode into the canyons to find and pick berries. But again her restlessness returned.

There was a bright spot on the dry and dusty landscape, however, and it was in Calgary. Guy Weadick and his wife were returning to Calgary and word spread that they planned to produce another stampede - the Victory Stampede – named in honour of the end of the war. Throughout the community people shared memories of the first stampede in 1912 and started to make plans to go to Calgary. An August horse sale and stampede were at least something to look forward to, and Bertha would not miss it.

Her plans were firm and she left Twin Butte for a reunion with Guy and Florence, but not a visit to the Pekisko ranch. Severe stomach pains a few days before the Stampede almost ended her plans and her life. The pains were bad enough that she went to the High River hospital, where she was diagnosed with acute appendicitis and immediately sent to the operating room. Whether she was officially discharged or left because she wanted to is not important. Bertha believed she had recovered and within a few days she was watching the parade on Main Street, Calgary, and the rodeo from the stands. As she soaked up the excitement, watching both men and women make great rides on great broncs, she wished she could be down there with them. How much more exciting it would be to move from being an observer to a competitor at one of these big shows. She decided that one day she would create a name for herself as a famous bronc rider!

Roy was in Calgary too. He was the wild card in her return to Alberta. How would she deal with her conflicting feelings – equal parts desire and dread? They saw each other in Twin Butte. They saw each other in Calgary. Could reconciliation really be possible between two independent, stubborn, unforgiving and deeply wounded individuals? It would not happen this time. They fought and failed to make peace.

Although her stay in Portland had been short, it had introduced Bertha to a wonderful, carefree lifestyle. She loved the city scene: the independence, the dances, the movies, a place of her own and the pay cheques. Her one reason to stay in Alberta - Roy - was no longer compelling. She found herself actually looking forward to life without him. So in September Bertha and Ingra took the train back to Oregon.

Back in Portland, Bertha easily slipped back into city life and settled into her place in the Carlos Apartment Building. The girls returned to their work at the Benson Hotel telephone switchboard. To make her new start more complete, Bertha created a new name. She adopted her middle name and left behind the hated Bertha. Her letter to Lala in January said: "Having a wonderful time here now – really living again. We are getting along OK. I am Marguritta here. Please send me my riding boots, breeches and mittens". Bertha had plans to ride again.

Because of the drought Alvin sold his sheep and cattle, and a few weeks later followed his sisters to the United States, moving to Washington to find work breaking horses. Johnny followed him, also looking for winter work. It was only four years since the Ekelunds' memorable family Christmas, with everyone together at the Twin Butte ranch. By the end of 1919 the family was scattered again: June lying in the Hillspring cemetery; Alvin and Johnny working in Washington; Bertha and Ingra living in Portland; Aron and family in Edmonton; and only Lala still in southern Alberta, married and working on her own ranch.

CHAPTER ELEVEN:
Wild West Show, 1920

Big rodeos became popular events in western towns and cities between 1910 and 1920. They drew huge crowds of people expecting to be entertained. After sitting as an observer at the Calgary Stampede just a few years ago, in 1920 Bertha decided to enter a similar big show close to Portland. This was her chance to live another dream.

Alvin was close by, in Washington, working on a large ranch. He was breaking horses and helping supply stock for the rodeos along the coast. In Portland, a five-day Wild West Show was held alongside the horse races. Events for both men and women were on the program.

Although many spectators considered rodeo events to be too dangerous for women, female competitors usually received the loudest cheers from the crowd. Bertha joined Alvin at the Race City Speedway Wild West Show. He entered the roping. She entered the bronc riding, the Roman riding (standing on the backs of two horses as they galloped over jumps and around the track) and the relay race. Bertha was excited to share the day with a number of well-recognized rodeo women. Each competitor hoped to make the best ride, but at the same time, each was happy to help the others out and cheer on a good performance.

It was a perfect, warm and clear August afternoon. At twenty-three, Bertha was confident and fearless. She had been riding her whole life and loved to take on the challenge of horses "with attitude". Because she was not a big woman, she had carefully selected her clothes: a bright striped shirt with the sleeves rolled up; a full buckskin split-skirt; her best tall boots; and the final touch, a big, wide-brim felt hat ... she was small, but she would be noticed! And she would put on a show for the crowd!

Roman riding was an event scheduled near the beginning of the day and Bertha found it an easy job to place one foot securely on the back of each horse and hold on tightly to the long reins. Good balance and a matched pair of horses allowed her to easily complete the jumps and the trip around the racetrack. It would be at another rodeo that her horses would run away and give her a good scare.

The Saddle Bronc Riding event was about mid-day and waiting for her first bronc seemed the hardest. She watched as her horse, a little bay with a dark mane and tail, was haltered and led out to the middle of the field. A cowboy on another horse snubbed the little bronc up to his saddle horn. Another man quickly threw the blindfold over its head. She helped Alvin throw her saddle on and they tightened the cinch. This should be easy – such a little horse and standing so quiet. Women were to ride with the stirrups tied below the horse's belly – in theory making it just a little easier to stay on – and often no one in the crowd even noticed. It was actually an insult to many of these women as they were just as capable and experienced as the men in the riding events.

The announcer called the next rider, after whom it would be Bertha's turn. Carefully she eased down onto the bronc's back and tucked her feet into the stirrups. She felt a little quiver from the small mare. She grabbed the reins and waited, enjoying the moment. She felt the warm sun on her back. The dust from the field tickled her nose as the smells of leather and horse sweat mixed together. She felt a shiver of excitement run up her spine, a nervous tension just before she nodded her head. She let the quiet respect from the men helping her soak in. "You ready?" they asked.

Bertha at Rose City Speedway Wild West Show, 1920

She barely heard the announcer's voice: "Our next rider is Texas Tommy!" he called. "Let'er buck!" came the cry as she nodded her big hat. The blindfold was pulled away and her little mare gave a jump and a kick and headed out onto the grass field. Bertha kept her feet forward and her arm in the air. She could hear the cheers from the crowd as the seconds ticked by. She matched the bronc jump for jump. And then - so quick - it was over. She jumped off, landed on her feet and gave a big wave of her hat to the crowd. The rodeo fans loved it!

It was not long before her second horse was led out and she was ready to ride again. The same thrill of excitement ran through her body as she climbed aboard. She had another small but wild horse and she matched this one similarly buck for buck and again made a great ride.

The next event was the relay race and this is when she ran into trouble. The relay was a real "western" event.[6] Each of the women competing had a string of horses to ride, tied to the rail at intervals around the racetrack. Mounted on their first horse at the start line, they would race at full speed around the first section of the track. They would charge into the change area, dismount, and jump onto the next horse. This manoeuver was repeated as many as five times along the racetrack, depending on the particular race. The first woman across the finish line on her final horse was declared the winner.

The danger came with each change. Horses charged into and out of the area; helpers untied horses and grabbed loose reins while the women leapt as quickly as possible from one mount to the next. The crowd loved the fast pace and excitement of the race, but the noise, the dust, the shouts and the commotion spooked many of the horses at the rail. They were nervous and scared.

Bertha got off to a good start and, as she was always fiercely competitive, she was out to win. She jumped off her first mount, threw the reins to Alvin and was on her second horse in seconds. She headed out on to the track and started toward the next corner. But this horse refused to turn, and at full speed ran straight into the fence, throwing her off. She landed hard on the other side of the fence and was out of the race.

Bertha before the relay race

"It was a bad wreck but she did not get hurt much," Alvin reported in a letter to Lala back in Alberta. As Alvin and Bertha were both taught never to complain and to get right back on the horse, ignoring any pain, we can only guess what it meant to be "not hurt much". She was tired and dirty at the end of the day, but still looking forward to doing it all again. Her family nickname, Tommy, seemed a perfect fit in this setting.

As she left the rodeo infield, a newspaper photographer from the *Portland Telegram* called her over. "Good ride young lady," he said. "Just stand here for a second so I can get your picture on the ground. I took a dandy of your ride. I want to publish it and I can get you copies by the end of the week. Where can I find you?"

Bertha gave him one of her sly smiles and tucked her hands behind her back for the photo. "I'll be looking for you – you won't have to find me," she grinned. "I want to send these pictures back to Alberta."

The next day, August 12th, 1920, a picture of Margaret Ekelund ("Texas Tommy"), "whose ability as a horsewoman was clearly demonstrated," appeared in the local paper.[7]

Bertha rode every day of that five-day Wild West Show and continued on to its next stop in Vancouver. The next year she joined the show

Margaret Ekelund ("Texas Tommy") in the *Portland Telegram* August 12th, 1920

again, and rode in Portland and Pendleton. She loved the thrill of the ride, the roar of the crowd, and the company of the other participants. She felt alive and free. And for a while, she and Alvin got along.

Bertha was a chameleon – celebrated one day as a country girl grinning from the back of a bronc and the next day as a city girl dancing the Charleston in a Portland club.

CHAPTER TWELVE:
"This certainly is the life I love"

Portland was an exciting place in the post-war era. Bertha and Ingra found themselves swept into a social whirlwind typical of the early Roaring Twenties. The young women loved the casual fashions of the day and eagerly purchased women's magazines to keep up with the latest trends. They were the picture of fashion in their slim flapper dresses and cloche hats, resembling as much as possible, the movie stars in the pictures.

Bertha favoured shoes with heels to add a few inches to her five-foot-three-inch frame. She searched for just the right accessories and put her sewing skills to use to make anything she couldn't find or afford. She recklessly spent her pay cheques on fashion and fun. The sisters loved joining their friends at parties, shows and clubs. Often out late, their biggest challenge was getting up and going to work in the morning. Bertha's life was full of variety. She had money to spend, and enjoyed buying all the little things that she wanted. She lived in the present and saw no need to save. She seemed happy and the months flew by.

Train travel was fast and easy, so most summers she took a trip back to Alberta for a visit. When Alvin moved back to the ranch, she found it hard not to go "home" too. Her Alberta roots were deep and strong. In 1923 she spent July, August and

September in Twin Butte, helping out with work on the ranch, sewing with Lala, and spending hours playing with her niece Nona, whom she called "Old Kidder". Her favourite horse, Buck, with a snorty disposition, was still there, and whenever she could, she would take him out for a ride and a tune-up.

Roy was in the area too, and occasionally they found themselves working side-by-side. As the days wore on, the conflict and bitterness that remained in their relationship escalated. By the end of the summer of 1923, decisions had been made to sever all ties. Bertha sold her cattle and they divided all their assets. Lala was to keep Buck, her saddle and her bridle, and was given strict instructions that Roy was "not to get his hands on them"! Bertha wanted nothing more to do with Roy Marshall. By the end of the summer she and Ingra were ready to go back to their city life.

When the girls' train pulled into the Portland station that September day, they were both filled with renewed hope and optimism - they were making a real break from their Alberta ties this time. Ingra was especially excited and nervous, as she was about to embark on a new chapter of her life. Guy Owen, a handsome Portland businessman, had asked her to marry him. The wedding took place on October 4th, 1923, with Bertha the only Ekelund family member present. Ingra was looking forward to a promising future, unaware of the few chances she would have to see her older sister, father and brothers again.

The young couple had a quick honeymoon and moved in with Guy's folks until they could establish themselves on their own. Soon they both returned to their jobs in Portland. Ingra was welcomed back by Bertha and the other girls in the telephone office and slipped into a routine of work six days a week. She was happy to have the 8 a.m. to 5 p.m. shift so she could be home to prepare a good hot dinner for her new husband. On the two days when she worked a split shift, from 9 a.m. to 1 p.m. and 5 p.m. to 9 p.m., she would stop by Bertha's apartment in the middle of the day. The girls still worked together and enjoyed time together. During the months of that fall, Ingra was very happy – she wrote to Lala:

> *Today is beautiful out; the sun is shining so bright and warm. It makes me think that life is truly beautiful and love grand.*

Ingra and Guy in front of their Portland home, circa 1924

Bertha had returned to Portland with cash in her pocket and wanted only to be free from Roy. She immediately initiated divorce proceedings and began gathering the necessary documentation. She was in control of her life. She settled in to her own little apartment and used her creativity and imagination to decorate it with her unique style. Again she asked Lala to send her a few things: two oak frames and two rugs.

Her cheerful letter in November, 1923, insensitively points out the differences between her life and that of her hard working older sister.

> *We have such a difficult life here. Shows and dances, parties at night and work every day each week […] I have been out every night this week as usual and have had a day off today all by myself – just to rest – this certainly is the life I love. I can stay up just as I like and no one to send me to bed, only I can't play the Victrole after ten at night but I do all of my hats and little jobs at night – wash hankies and socks read the Cosmo and private things to my own liking […] I do get homesick for the happenings around there (in Alberta) when I stop and think a minute. I have not heard from Roy yet. Suppose he is still in Montana. He has never returned the paper to be signed yet either let me know if you have heard of him being around there lately. He certainly causes me no end of trouble.*
>
> *Thanks so much for the paper you signed.*
> *It was ok all of that helps you see. I*
> *have to have proof of everything.*

Always looking for something new, she registered for a beauty culture course. In February 1924, Marguriette Marshall completed Madam Patteneaude's System of Beauty Culture at the Pacific School of Beauty Culture in Portland. The graduation certificate exists, but, curiously, it is not signed by the school.

While she was taking this course she moved again and lived temporarily with the relative of another man she had met, Hector or "Spaghetti" as she called him.

Bertha still loved to flirt and tease men who showed any interest, but she was not really looking for another entanglement. However, one man seemed to catch her attention more than the others. Dave Wells was a test pilot who had spent time in France during the war. She called him "my Aviator". He had returned to Portland from the war and worked as a mechanic and shop foreman at the Portland Packard dealership. Dave and Roy were different in almost every way; where Roy was tall and lean, Dave was just a bit taller than Bertha, who stood at five feet three inches when she stood as straight as possible; Roy was a wizard with animals while Dave could fix anything with a motor; Roy couldn't have sung if his life depended on it, and Dave was a musician who played a mean saxophone.

Bertha began to accept Dave's increasing invitations for a night out on the town, and they spent more and more time together. But this time Bertha was not an inexperienced teenager; this time she enjoyed a three-year courtship.

Bertha's attraction to Dave was real. She had filed for divorce from Roy, but Roy was being very slow in signing and returning the required papers. She waited impatiently for four months, until finally, though no signed papers came, Bertha married Dave Wells in March of 1924. She believed that it was wrong for the men of the Mormon Church to have multiple wives, but for her, a modern woman, it was acceptable to have two husbands, especially if you were in the process of divorcing the first one.

Dave Wells Portland, 1924

It seemed that Bertha had actually found happiness, but unfortunately for her, nothing in her life seemed to remain stable for long. Her next move was to San Francisco with Dave. They were together only a few months. Another photo, taken in May of the next year, documented the day that they separated and Dave left. Bertha and Dave kept in touch with letters and occasional visits, but they were not suited for life together.

Still wanting to be free from Roy, who had not responded to any of her requests, she was able to obtain an Interlocutory Decree of Divorce in California, dated April 8th, 1925, from Roy Marshall on the grounds of "the defendant's wilful desertion and wilful neglect". She was required to wait one full year for the divorce to become final.

CHAPTER THIRTEEN:
"Sure, I want to be with my relatives for a change"

Meanwhile, Ingra was building her life in Portland with Guy. They now had their own apartment and she had exciting news to share with her Alberta family. She wrote in March that she was expecting their first child. The baby was born in September 1924, and Ingra wrote to Lala while still in the comfort and care of the Wilson Memorial Hospital:

> *Now I will try to explain everything to you folks and about my new experiences. First of all Baby Guy came four weeks too early; we had expected him October 16th so of course that made things altogether different. We were awfully surprised when the doctor gave me the examination and said to be at the hospital by 8 o'clock. The labor pains started Saturday morning at 1 AM and lasted until Sunday 4:15 AM – making 27 hours all told. Junior was born Sunday, Sept. 14th and weighed only 6 pounds […] I haven't any pains, (anywhere) pulse and temperature normal and with a very keen appetite – guess I'm all O.K. now.*

> *Daddy Guy is the proudest new daddy you ever did see. He just grins and grins [...]* <u>*We are both very happy and love our baby more than anything in the world [...]*</u> *The Doctor tells me I can leave here this coming Saturday. That means I will be here 14 days. That's a long time but as the case was pre-mature he can't let me go home sooner.*

In contrast, Lala's birthing experience that following spring was almost fatal. She had spent the winter at her homestead cabin with six-year-old Nona. Her husband, Jack, was in Vancouver recovering from panniculitis (an inflammatory disorder that is treated with a long period of rest). Lala's occasional help came from her father, Nels. It had been a difficult pregnancy and Lala suffered with sore and swollen legs that limited her mobility. The baby, whom they hoped would be a boy, was due in early April, and Lala planned to get to Pincher Creek and have the baby in the hospital. Jack planned to be home in plenty of time for the birth. But an unexpected March snowstorm changed everything.

When Lala realized that it was time to get to Pincher Creek, she, little Nona and Nels packed and readied the wagon to drive to town. But a severe and swift storm had left choking drifts of snow and roads that were muddy and almost impassable. It took them hours to travel only four miles to brother Aron's house, where they realized that they would be able to go no further.

Lala went in to labour and quick decisions had to be made. She was made comfortable and two neighbours were called to come and help. Both women had experience as midwives, and with common sense and efficiency they eased Lala through a difficult birth. They delivered a healthy baby girl, just a few weeks premature. But Lala was exhausted and weak and started to hemorrhage. The nearest doctor, an unreliable character with a love of whiskey, was thirty miles away. He was summoned using the closet phone in Twin Butte, and he agreed to come on the condition that his fees include at least one bottle of whiskey. He was their only choice.

More frantic phone calls were made and arrangements put in place for one team and buggy to take the doctor the first fifteen miles and a second team to be waiting to complete the remainder of the journey.

As they waited for the doctor, Lala's midwives realized that they must stop the bleeding immediately or they would lose her. They used an old home remedy – ergot. (Although illegal, controlled doses of ergot have been used since the middle ages to control maternal bleeding after childbirth. Where it came from on that April day remains a mystery, but it was the only thing that saved Lala from death.) When the doctor finally stumbled into the room drunk, angry, and too late to be of any help, he was furious. He criticized the actions of the women, gave Lala a quick examination and was soon on his way back to town. No one was sorry to see him go.

Jack arrived in Pincher Creek the next day, tired from his long trip from Vancouver, and was quickly told the news of the birth of his second daughter, and the scare they had had with Lala. He immediately headed to Aron's home, happy and relieved to be reunited with his wife and two daughters. Once Lala had regained her strength, Jack moved his family back to their ranch. Lala was still weak and tired, but she did not get the luxury of fourteen days of hospital care and pampering. There was work to be done as soon as she returned home.

Lala wrote to her sister telling her that the new baby would be named Inga Ada, after her aunt and her grandmother. Ingra wrote back:

> *Surely I don't object to my name and I'll be glad to have a little name sake […] I wish that I could come up to T.B. [Twin Butte] this summer and bring Jr., so that you folks could see him, and so that we could see little baby, sister Nona and you folks. Sure want to be with my relatives for a change but there is no hope until next summer.*

She desperately wanted to introduce her baby to her family. She was feeling increasingly homesick and lonely and neglected, as is suggested in her December letter to Lala:

> *Guy is getting to be a regular old granddad. He doesn't pay any attention to me anymore; it's just the baby he seems to care for.*

While her sisters were facing the challenges of husbands and babies, Bertha found herself alone in San Francisco. She found work in a beauty shop (her beauty culture course proved useful to her a number of times during her life). She worked there for almost a year, keeping up with the new styles and charming her clients. She waited for the mail every day and hoped for news from her sisters. She was anxious to see her new niece and nephew and sent her love to them in every letter. These letters, which travelled almost weekly between the three sisters, kept their bond strong.

And then an opportunity arose for Ingra: a trip to San Francisco! A chance to see Bertha! Ingra jumped at the opportunity to take the three-day ferry trip down the coast. She was excited but nervous about travelling with an eight-month-old baby, and about being seasick. She did report to Lala that she "sure fed the fish the first night". The trip was possible thanks to Guy's sister and young daughter, who were travelling by boat to return to their home near San Francisco and who had invited Ingra and Guy Jr. to join them.

The timing of the visit was perfect. Bertha's shop had recently been sold so she was free from work and could enjoy every minute of their time together. The sisters revelled in giggling, gossiping, sewing and catching up. Bertha instantly fell in love with her new nephew, whom she described as "just the darling […] all smiles and such a good kid." He was "so fat and so cute". She catered to his every whim.

Ingra outwardly objected that Bertha would spoil the baby but was actually happy to be given the attention and affection. Ingra and Guy Jr. vacationed in California from the middle of May to almost the end of June - a full six weeks - and Ingra loved every minute of it. She wrote to Lala, "Am enjoying San Francisco immensely".

It was a wonderful break for Ingra. And when it was time to return home, Bertha travelled with her back to Portland and then went on to Alberta to see the rest of the family. She spent most of her time with Lala and her two nieces. Bertha really loved the children; she would hold them, tease them, give them forbidden treats, and threaten to take them home with her. She kept her lost opportunity to be a mother buried deep in her heart, and lavished her sisters' children with all of her affection.

With nothing to tie her down, Bertha allowed her Alberta visit to last for several months. Then she travelled back to Portland and stayed on for Christmas with Ingra and her family. There she reconnected with many friends and a few old beaus who continued to give her handsome Christmas gifts and optimistically promised to take her away with them on their next "holiday". One such special friend, Hector, listened to her lament that she had no job and no future. He had an idea, and together they hatched a plan for her to find a job in the San Francisco area; she needed a nursing certificate and an introduction to a medical specialist. Hector arranged for both. With these in place, she again boarded the Pacific Steamship Company ferry to San Francisco and on to Los Gatos. Optimistic again, she wrote to Lala describing the fun she and Hector had on the voyage, and signed her name jauntily as "Salty B!"

Ingra was left behind again as Bertha embarked on her next adventures. Ingra still desperately wanted to travel to Alberta, but she did not have the choices that were open to Bertha. She felt that it was impossible for her to leave Portland, even for a short visit. Guy Sr. had taken on new business responsibilities and was working twelve- and fourteen-hour days. He had no time for holidays. In every letter she told her sisters how baby Guy was a busy happy boy and how he was the focus of her life. Ingra fondly remembered her last time at home, picking berries with her sisters in Blind Canyon, now two years ago. As her twenty-fifth birthday approached she wrote to Lala, "I don't mind telling you all that from now on – I'm forgetting about my birthdays, 'cause I'm ¼ of a century old now, and I'll tell the world I'm not keen about getting any older."

Another letter reveals how she hoped to get her slim figure back after the baby was born, and her interest in new ideas; Ingra attended an interesting lecture and reported that Mme. Sheaufnau spoke about "Reducing". She told the women to "diet – eat herring, gluetin[sic] bread, buttermilk, raw tomatoes, lamb chops, pineapple and then take Epsom salt baths every night". She guaranteed this would "take off fifteen to thirty pounds in one month". These were new concepts at that time, but forecast our obsessive modern search for the perfect weight-loss recipe.

Busy months passed for the young mother as she tried to keep up with a very active child and support her ambitious husband. Letters could travel for her and she told Lala more about Guy Jr.: "Everyone that sees him says they have never seen a baby with so much pep and one that is on the go so much […] he has the bluest eyes you ever saw – not light blue nor dark – just pretty clear blue."

She told everyone how proud she was of him as he learned to walk and to talk. She worried about his health and his manners, as all mothers do, and sent Lala suggestions for feeding her daughters. She recommended an English gruel called Robinson's Groats, "for babies and mothers, that cost 60 cents per pound tin. Awfully good and just the thing to put with cow milk."

By the next spring, 1926, the Owen family was planning another move. They bought a new place with an old house and two lots and made plans to design and build a new home the following year. That meant that there were even more expenses to worry about. Guy Sr. was finally working for himself, but his hours were even longer. Ingra looked forward to letters from her family as she occasionally got "terribly lonesome":

[E]very once in a while I get the blues and a letter always cheers me up [...] some days I get so lonesome for all you folks that I just feel miserable. Wish you could live down here for a while.

Finally, in the spring of 1927, Ingra and Guy Jr. did find a way to go to Alberta for a visit. Bertha decided to travel with them and it was a delightful reunion when the three sisters and the three children were finally together. They talked and laughed, and shared stories, jokes, recipes and treatments. They watched the cousins play together and hoped to see this scene repeated many times over the years. But for Ingra it would be her last reunion.

Sisters and cousins:
(Left to right) Lala with Guy, Ingra with Inga, Nona and Bertha
Twin Butte, 1927

Each of the next two winters Ingra planned and hoped to arrange another visit to Alberta, even putting a bit of money aside to make it possible. And each year there was some reason or obstacle that prevented the trip.

In every letter she repeated her longing to spend time with her sister and her nieces. Her health was fragile. Her "blues" intensified. Her depression increased. She suspected that her husband was not faithful. In April of 1929 she wrote:

> *I have been very sick […] we just had to get a car so that I could get out on Sundays or on a nice afternoon. I know I shall feel better now and get an appetite. Can't eat a thing […] I sure would love to see [Nona] and Inga – all of you in fact.*

Three months later, on July 12th, 1929, Ingra left her son with a neighbour, went home and drank carbolic acid. She was found by her husband when he came home from work. She was only twenty-eight years old. Lala travelled alone to Portland to help her brother-in-law bury his wife, her sister. Once again a small child watched his mother's coffin being lowered into the ground. The shame of suicide was quickly covered up back in Alberta. Friends and relatives were told that Ingra had been sick. The Ekelund family lived with another tragic and unexpected loss.

And Bertha had disappeared.

Ingra Matilda Owen, circa 1927

CHAPTER FOURTEEN:
"Make believe - even if you don't know"

The Oaks Sanitarium in Los Gatos California, just south of San Francisco, opened in 1910. It was a small private facility for patients who could afford the twenty to thirty dollars per week fee. Protected by the Santa Cruz Mountains to the east, it sat on an open hillside surrounded by trees and shrubs. The facility boasted spacious white buildings with large windows on all sides and open, airy and sun filled rooms. Several small houses dotted the area and were available for patients and/or staff to occupy. The buildings, surroundings, and landscaped grounds created a true oasis for those suffering from tuberculosis.

The new nurse at the Oaks Sanitarium, Marge, arrived on January 13th 1926, and began work immediately. She had fourteen patients assigned to her. Dr. Voorsanger, the Medical Director, and Dr. Alexander, the Assistant Medical Director, both spoke very highly of her. Her diploma from Pittsburgh, Pennsylvania, dated March 23rd 1925, confirmed that she had recently completed a three-year course of theoretical and practical instruction in the medical, surgical and obstetrical departments of the institution. She took great pride in her starched white uniform and crisp white nurse's cap. She was obviously a trained and efficient young professional.

Bertha Marshall, a.k.a Margaretta (Marge) Shirley Randolf
Oaks Sanatorium Los Gatos California, 1926

"Marge" was younger than most of the nurses on staff. Many had been at the Oaks Sanitarium for years. A petite young woman (only twenty-seven years old), she was full of energy, and quick with a smile. This engaging redhead was quickly accepted into the hospital community. The patients liked her, and she was competent and quick to learn details of the treatments required. She was efficient and accurate in administering medications. Her notes on the charts were carefully and clearly written. She kept a small notebook in her pocket and conscientiously made notes of important points. She was often seen reviewing her medical texts in her spare time, usually chewing on a few carrots.

She wrote home to her sister Lala:

> [...]and now here I am down at Los Gatos in the Santa Cruz mountains and oH! away high up in the Red Woods too; the ideal spot and in a TB Sanitarium at last but now don't take it as a shock because I have not got tuberculosis. oH! but am one of the gang of 6 nurses and on regular duty.
>
> So you think it queer that the Dr. A and Dr Voorsanger let me in as a trained nurse. Well I have done worse things with men - and got away with it - why worry about such small things as what you are. & I got a little training in Port and I have a lot more here now and where they specialize in TB, well there are just certain things that have to be done not like in a Hosp where they <u>do</u> everything. I know the different subs [?] and dressings and cough mix and how to file charts and feed the nourishments and that is all that is really necessary. I will be a specialist on TB when I leave here. I study on it every minute I have time. Book in my pocket for notes & I never miss. It's just a trick and I have learned it a long time ago. That's - make believe even if you don't know.

I have the most preferable position on the route now. I get my work done easy and quick & Dr. A said he would put me into the Office next. <u>That is</u> in charge of the Emergency calls. The charting for 96 patients. The Laboratory – mixing cough mix and Gargles and Rubs you know for sweat and pain and they are chiefly Formulas […] and alcohol just different proportions. Then the tablets to be given out for each and Iodine for painting shoulders and chests. Charge of the little opr room where the patients come in for their weekly opr, which consists chiefly of Numo Thorax & X-Ray. It is very interesting in fact I am simply crazy about it now. Everyone is so kind to me here and I get on with them all even the old house keeper she is a severe crank.

But Oh! It is perfectly lovely here […] I know you must worry about what I am doing and all. But if you saw me sit at ease and have old Heck drive me and call for me and put me around with the dandy pay check <u>clear</u> you would not worry at all. I have more nerve sometimes than a brass monkey. I came here as a trained nurse and no one but the Dr. A does not know that I am not and I surely put on the Dog for them too. You would take a whole glass of epsom salts if I told you. oH! I have to laugh when I come off duty in the evenings and say if you don't think the little old diary has some funny things in it now.

With help from her good friend Hector Pichette, who she called Spaghetti, and a forged nursing diploma, Bertha had found a new identity and a new career. For the next two years she merrily worked at the sanatorium, writing her charts "backhand", dying her hair with henna and egg so the red hair would accentuate the white cap and uniform, eating carrots (as she believed they would keep her healthy) and taking full advantage of her new persona. She believed that she had succeeded with a "few brains and passable looks but it is my disposition that wins for me and I am truly happy now." Many men at the sanatorium noticed the young nurse and complimented her, not only on her good work, but also on her good looks.

She loved the warm winter weather, the green of the hills after rain, the spring blossoms and the gentle winds. She felt the lurking black depression retreat and with it a surge of optimism and hope. With a "clear heart and mind again" she felt she had landed in paradise. One letter was written "from the top of the world", after a strenuous, solitary three-hour hike to the top of one of the Santa Cruz mountains. She sat looking over the valley, watching the sunset and acknowledging that she had reached a peak, not only physically, but emotionally and mentally as well. The beauty of this sunset she compared to the beauty of a sunset in Pekisko; the peace of this moment she contrasted with the turmoil of that winter.

Bertha (or Marge as she was known there) became fast friends with many of the nurses, sharing jokes and wine in her room while she did their hair and they told her stories. She describes her co-workers to Lala:

> [A] funny bunch of nurses [...] they are all better looking than myself and they <u>know</u> something - all

> *older and all had plenty of husbands of different nationalities and creed and occupation. I don't tell them of my experiences and they call me The Kid sometimes I do get a real kick out of playing the Innocent. Dr. A asks them to be careful of their language in front of me [...] one drinks wine - one smokes and one uses Snuff and the other has been a real nervous breakdown.*

These nurses were a lively group and Bertha enjoyed their company. She found their jokes and medical stories to be quite shocking and told Lala that they would make her blush. She was getting an education that extended beyond the fences of her limited childhood experiences, the teachings of the Mormon Church, and the traditional values of a rural ranching community.

April 8th, 1926 was a day she had really been looking forward to. After the required year of waiting, her final decree of divorce from Roy Marshall was settled by the California court. She was given legal permission to resume the name of Margaretta Shirley Randolph. She was legally free from Roy and the detested name of Bertha. In January 1927 she wrote to Lala:

> *Landed here one year on the 13th and have surely gotten along famously – have a hankering for adventure Spaghetti giving gifts – I do not think anyone will trap me again. I surely will keep my guard up [...] I just would not anex [sic] myself to that detestable name of Brita Ekelund – just address me as Shirley M. Randolf. I wrote the*

*old Bossman (Alvin) a letter for Xmas and
Dave – or Lieutenant Wells I should say.*

The letters she sent to Alberta told how busy she was and were full of stories of work and of work-related adventures. They were often written quickly between frequent interruptions during her shifts and occasionally seemed confusing. They revealed a second dimension of her life in California, as the companion of a wealthy Italian businessman.

Hector Picchetti, the fourth son of Italian immigrants, was born in California in 1891. He grew up on a San Jose farm and vineyard established by his family. Vicenzo Picchetti, Hector's father, died in 1904 when Hector was just thirteen. The oldest boys in the family took over the vineyard, which continues to run today. The two younger boys, Atillio and Hector, stayed with their mother, Theresa, and their Aunt Louisa, and in 1921 moved to San Jose. Hector was then twenty-nine.

Neither of the younger brothers ever married. Hector went on to become a successful businessman and worked with his brother Atillio who owned a garage, buying, selling and fixing cars. With a spirit of adventure and an eye for opportunity, Hector sailed to Europe in 1922 and visited a variety of countries, including Italy. He was the only member of his family to travel back to Europe. He was a short, dark Italian with a boyish smile, money, power and daring. Hector resembled Roy Marshall in only one way: he was willing to break the rules if the opportunity arose and the outcome was in his favour.

They were a dangerous couple. Hector was intrigued by Bertha. She was smart, sexy, fearless and fun. He called her Marge. She called him Spaghetti.

Hector Picchetti California April 12, 1925

He loved her free spirit and encouraged her deceptions. She was willing to go along with any adventures that were suggested. Hector picked her up after work on a regular basis. He always had a new and expensive car and would whisk her away to Santa Cruz or San Jose or Salinas. He took her to expensive hotels, and they were seen at a selection of exclusive French and Italian restaurants. They joined Hector's brother Attilio and their many friends to attend shows and parties. Bertha was proud to report to Lala that "Marshall was the best dressed girl there."

> Well you know that I love to be dressed nice and I had the grandest silver diner [sic] dress, low cut beautiful – what there was of it but very plain just "plain silver" made in Paris. oH! – I have been here just one year without a break yesterday. No reputation here that I have in Canada – when I have the grandest sweetheart in the world for one year – he has been as faithful as Old Dog Tray.

Hector showered her with lavish gifts and sent her shopping with extra cash while he attended "meetings". The Picchettis' had some wonderful thoroughbred horses at their family ranch and because Bertha was eager to saddle and ride the horses, Hector bought her a lovely new white riding habit.

Hector's money opened the door to many exclusive experiences and he never hesitated to spend it on making Bertha happy. They stayed at the Robber's Roost, a ranch in Polo Pana, and tried target shooting with a .22 rifle, something Bertha was surprisingly good at. They floated lazily in the little boats on the water, and they indulged in the lovely meals at the ranch house.

They spent ten days on a break at the Isabel Grove Country Club relaxing on the beach and racing over the waves in a friend's speedboat "at 170 miles per hour!" Bertha called it recreation, and for her it made the routine of working for a whole week bearable. She felt "like a million dollars".

Bertha learned to drive, and her impulsive, reckless attitude was particularly in evidence:

> *I can drive fairly well now in traffic. I have only been picked up once for speeding, once for running through a safety zone, and once for not having a driving license in my name [...] I just about keep (Hector) broke paying the bills and keeping me out of jail – the Sherriff came out to take me into S F last week and had it not been for Hector and a speedy car I would have lost my position [...] but money and pull is everything in California.*

Often when it was time for Bertha to go back to the sanatorium the couple would take their time and explore all the small back roads and trails, discovering remote lakes and fishing spots. These many leisurely drives returning Bertha to work provided them with the knowledge to have an escape route when needed. Hector was the one Bertha could depend on to get her out of trouble.

Bertha thoroughly enjoyed her relationship with Hector and referred to it as "Italian Love". She was having great fun with the situation just as it was and did not want to complicate things. She was determined not to ruin it and create a new enemy by considering marriage. So she convinced herself that "Californians don't marry."

And she did not limit her friendships to her Italian lover. She was friendly with many people: there were her Alaskan friends, one of whom ("D.F.A.") presented her with a Christmas gift – "a grand necklace of real old Ivory beads made from the genuine Walrus Tusk"; the local florist always saved her a gardenia; the Chef would cook the fish she caught for her breakfast; she even flirted with the priests.

The third major facet of this complex woman was her unbreakable tie to Alberta and her family. She was always scribbling a letter. She waited impatiently for the mail and poured over every letter she received from her family. She worried and scolded them when she found out that Lala was experiencing continuous indigestion. She sent medical advice and had suggestions for possible ways to ease the discomfort, and encouraged her sister to find a good doctor in Calgary. She even offered to drop everything and come back and take care of her sister. She was cross with her father and brothers for not taking better care of Lala and themselves.

She wrote to Ingra to learn about her nephew, Guy Jr., and their new home in Portland. She always asked about her nieces and nephew, sending them her love and kisses, and wishing she could spend more time with them. When Alvin came to California to see a Wild West Show in September, she found a way to join him and they reminisced about the old days when they had been participants. As expected, when Alvin saw her, he tried to talk her into coming home. She refused. These two siblings were like firecrackers – quiet and safe before the fuse was lit but dangerous once ignited. This time there were not enough sparks to set off an argument.

When Hector was away, she was lonely. She wrote home:

I wish I could come home but I can't so that's that. My California Sweetheart is to return tonight from Chicago. He has been there two weeks – I have been the sewingest person you ever saw. <u>Seven</u> uniforms cut out and two nearly finished – I made some when I came here a year ago – Boss always says come home Tommy but I just cannot […] I often remember what Dad told me when I ran off with Moose "I made my own bed and must lie in it" and I guess I have. But I cannot come back to Alberta. It would be the same old story.

Her family's letters reignited memories of her love of the western lifestyle: the freedom of the ranching life; the thrill of climbing on a good horse; and the independence that could not be found when tied to shift work and nursing. She mentioned that Roy was with her in her dreams. She reminded herself that she couldn't/shouldn't/wouldn't go home, but the pull was very strong.

In the spring of 1927, when Ingra and baby Guy were finally taking their much longed for trip to Alberta, Bertha (a.k.a Marge(y) Marshall, a.k.a Shirley Randolph) decided to go home as well – for a visit. She had been nursing for a long year and was ready for a break. Work was becoming routine and the rigid shift work schedule was stifling to her. Maintaining the deception was also becoming more difficult. The police had come to the sanitarium to look for her. With Hector's help, "a speedy car and plenty of cash" she had evaded them, but she knew this could not last forever. People were getting suspicious about her story and her behaviour. She was getting homesick and romanticising her relationship with Roy. She remembered the good times and suppressed the conflicts and pain.

She joined Ingra and baby Guy on their trip to Alberta. Together again, the sisters had a most wonderful reunion and spent hours catching up and delighting in the joy of being together. They only had a few weeks together. It was not long enough. Going back to Los Gatos and Portland respectively was difficult for Bertha and Ingra, though in different ways. Ingra had no idea when she might return to the Alberta foothills. Bertha knew that her real home was not in California, and that changes were coming.

Unrealistically, Bertha believed that she had been healed by the California sunshine and warm climate. She believed that after more than a year without the black depression and impulsive rage, it would never return. She convinced herself that she could move back to Alberta and remain happy, and that her old problems would not re-emerge. She was a country girl at heart, and her visit to Alberta had confirmed that she was ready to return.

Bertha was only back in California long enough to gather her things and say goodbye to her friends and patients. She left Hector, promising to keep in touch. Within a few weeks of her return to Los Gatos, she had resigned from her job, packed her belongings, and moved back to the Alberta foothills.

The woman who came back had changed, at least outwardly. At twenty-nine, she appeared confident and carefree, though she had retained her impulsive nature, her poor judgement and quick temper, as would become evident. She had convinced herself that rules were meant for everyone but her, in particular because she had been successful in her many deceptions. However moving from the relaxed California coast, where she could disappear into the city crowds, to a traditional community in which everyone knew everyone and maintained entrenched and traditional values would present Bertha with greater challenges than she ever expected.

CHAPTER FIFTEEN:

"An unsettled life"

Bertha returned to a community of curious and often critical people who were convinced that she remained a maverick – unpredictable and unconventional. It was not long before neighbours were talking about her behavior and the rumours spread about her escapades in California, her flirting and/or impertinence with local men, and her divorce from Roy. The gossip grew when she and Roy were seen together. At first she stayed with either Alvin or Lala, but that soon felt too restrictive. She was used to being free and independent, and she wanted a place of her own.

Bertha and Roy could not help but encounter each other in such a small rural community. They would see each other at the post office, or at local dances, or even at family gatherings. It was not long before the old magnetism re-emerged, as at least some of the hurt had been forgotten. They decided to try once more to live together.

Bertha was optimistic but not realistic. She had Roy back. He was a handsome and charming man. He had convinced her that he had missed her terribly and was willing to change his ways. She was flattered and sure that she would be enticing enough to keep him away from his old habits of gambling and womanizing. Both Bertha and Roy acknowledged that their relationship had failed before, but they wanted to make it work this time. They were drawn to each other with an elastic tension that had survived time and distance. The close times were passionate and intimate. The disagreements that pushed them apart were equally passionate, and destructive. Subject to endless community gossip, and under the critical gaze of both her older brother Alvin and the elders of the Mormon Church, they decided to find some peace by claiming to re-marry. This was the beginning of a turbulent twenty months.

The couple rented a small place west of Hillspring only a few miles from Alvin's ranch. They had a few pigs and sheep, chickens and cows and of course, horses. Sometimes they had an old car to use; other times a wagon and team. They travelled back and forth to Alvin and Lala's ranches to help out with all work that needed to be done: feeding the stock; trapping and hunting for food; cutting wood to keep the homes warm. Bertha and her siblings supported each other as they fought the strong winds, the deep snow, and freezing temperatures. The winter of 1928 proved to be an unusually long and bitter one with cold and snow lasting well into April. Ranchers ran out of feed for the sheep more than once and watched many lambs die in the spring storms. Everyone in the family worked hard, and there was little money to be earned from their long hours.

Only a short distance away, the Waterton Park village had grown and become a busy summer community. Now there was a post office, government buildings, a restaurant, a dance hall and hotels. The American Great Northern Railway had identified an opportunity to lure Americans north of the border during the prohibition era. Two years were spent building the Prince of Wales Hotel, which opened in July 1927. This grand hotel, designed to resemble a Swiss chalet, was situated on a windy bluff with a spectacular view of the lakes. Its interior replicated a traditional British country manor, with high tea served in the afternoon.

Alvin quickly saw new possibilities for business. He negotiated through the spring to obtain the contract to supply the new hotel's restaurant with meat for the summer season. Deliveries of lamb, veal and pork started in June and continued as orders came in through the summer. Alvin was paid twenty-five cents per pound.

The long winter had been hard on the Marshalls' fragile relationship and by spring Bertha was looking for a reason to leave Hillspring and Roy. Alvin knew that they were "not getting along again". And he also knew that one of their biggest problems was a lack of money. He suggested that Bertha talk to Captain Harrison, the manager, about working in the restaurant at the Prince of Wales Hotel. She applied immediately and was hired as a waitress. Bertha was excited about the chance to return to Waterton, her childhood playground. She moved into her father's log cabin in the center of the village. Meanwhile, Roy headed in the opposite direction, to Lethbridge, to also seek work.

Once again Bertha donned a crisp white uniform, but this time she could replace the stiff nurse's cap with a stylish broad white headband and get rid of the white stockings. She enjoyed the challenge of starting yet another new career. The American tourists that came on the bus from Montana were curious, and she had great fun telling them stories of the dangers of the Canadian wilderness and the fierce animals that were lurking just outside the door.

Captain Harrison appreciated her quick wit, her sense of humour and her customer service, and after only a few weeks on the job she was promoted to head waitress. That put her in charge of the main dining room, and the supervision of the other waitresses. Bertha didn't mind the long hours or the hard work, and she expected everyone else to have the same attitude. She was seen as an effective manager, but there were times when her impatience and quick temper caused problems with the other girls. Many did not like their temperamental boss. She worked at the hotel for the summer and fall season of 1928.

The greatest appeal of Waterton for Bertha was the mountains that surround the town. When not at work, she was on horseback, re-riding the trails to the canyons, hidden lakes and waterfalls she'd explored as a youth, often accompanied by one or more of the young park wardens. She enjoyed riding one particular horse that she described as "a mean horse but grand to ride on the trail".

The second attraction was the social life. She had regained her freedom and independence. The weekend dances at the

Bertha in her white California riding habit, a gift from Hector, Waterton Alberta, 1928

pavilion were well attended by locals and tourists, and Bertha loved to dance until the notes of the last waltz faded. Tension with Roy eased and she permitted his occasional visits to her cabin. They were seen together at some of the weekend dances.

At the end of September, Bertha returned to Hillspring and another winter with Roy. And all the old problems returned with her. Her lurking depression resurfaced and her simmering anger erupted. She fought with Roy. She fought with Alvin. She caused no end of worry for Lala. She reached a breaking point with Roy and moved to Alvin's ranch, but this too was soon an impossible situation. Bertha and Alvin argued about almost everything.

Things came to a head in a dispute over the ownership of a flock of sheep. Alvin and Bertha had worked together to round up the animals. Bertha felt that Alvin had not paid her fairly over the winter and claimed that the sheep were hers. When it was time to confirm where they were to go next, Alvin and Bertha had different plans: Alvin planned to move them to a new pasture, while Bertha planned to take them to market

She sat squarely on her horse and stared straight up into Alvin's eyes. "These are my sheep. We have worked for them. I own them and I intend to take them."

Alvin's horse took a small step but he checked it and returned the stare. "By the hell woman! They stay here."

Recklessly, Bertha reached down and snatched the small pistol that she always carried out of her pocket, levelled it at Alvin for just an instant, then dropped her aim and shot his faithful sheepdog. It was a good shot; the dog died instantly.

She saw shock and rage on Alvin's face. Immediately, she realized that she had overstepped the line, yet again. Alvin's fury was intense and his language colorful, accusing Bertha of trying to kill him. He informed her that he would report the incident to the police.

Bertha quietly but quickly rounded up her sheep and started to move them to her pasture. Alvin sat motionless behind her, already planning his report to the Pincher Creek police.

Bertha got her sheep, but at what cost? Roy was no help when she told him what she had done. She had created this mess and she would have to deal with it. Lala was shaken but not surprised. Bertha's behaviour for the last few weeks had been increasingly difficult to understand.

The next day Alvin was at the police station in Pincher Creek, where he reported that Bertha Marshall had pulled a gun on him and tried to kill him. The report was taken seriously and Constable Cawsey went out to Twin Butte to summon Bertha to appear in court. She was stunned. Alvin *had* reported the incident! She would have to face the court and the community ridicule! The constable met with a very angry woman who tried to convince him that she had done nothing wrong. He stood his ground in the face of her fury and eventually she realized that she had no choice. She reluctantly agreed to attend the hearing. The constable returned to town.

Bertha's anger was joined by self-pity and humiliation. She was already the subject of a great deal of gossip in the community, and this would only escalate in the next few weeks. She wavered between getting even and getting away. As her black depression darkened further, she took action.

The morning of the hearing, Bertha saddled her horse, slipped a sharp knife into her saddlebag, and without a word to anyone rode west toward Spread Eagle Mountain. It was mid-May and she could see that a spring storm was brewing over the mountains. The west wind was blowing.

As she rode on the temperature began to drop and first rain, then snow, started to fall. Bertha moved on, paying little attention to the cold and wind. She followed the trail up into a canyon and, as darkness came, she took out the little knife and made a deep gash into her wrist. The dark red blood splashed onto the new white snow. Tears fell down her cheeks as she ignored the pain in her wrist, hoping to find release from the pain in her heart. Blackness overtook her and she collapsed into a troubled sleep.

Hours passed and the blanket of snow got deeper and the temperature continued to fall. The bleeding on her wrist slowed and stopped as the cold temperature was nature's perfect first aid treatment. The hours ticked by. Eventually Bertha, confused, disoriented, and weak, realized that she was not dead or even dying, but that she was very cold and very uncomfortable. Slowly she acknowledged that she did not want to die and that her situation was serious. She knew that she needed help. She realized that she wanted to live; she wanted the baby she was carrying to live. Through the next two days and long dark nights she called and called for help, but only the animals of the forest could hear the calls that became weaker and weaker. Bertha slipped into unconsciousness again.

When Bertha did not appear at the hearing, the police travelled to Alvin's ranch to bring her in. Alvin, noticing that her horse was gone and suspecting that in her desperate and unhappy state she may have made a lethal choice, called on friends and neighbours to help search for her. The police joined the search, which lasted four long days.

At the head of the canyon, Bertha was found, barely conscious and very weak. She had been saved by the winter weather. Although she had lost a good deal of blood, the cold temperatures had slowed the flow and closed the wound on her wrist, saving her from death.

She was taken to Lala's house to be warmed and cared for. She was placed in the small room that belonged to her nieces in the Bechtel's little home, and Lala comforted her and cared for her.

"What's wrong with Auntie? Why does she move so slow?" Nona was confused about her usually fun loving aunt, who was always quick to play and to tease. Now she just stayed in bed. She was tearful … she seemed sick. Lala reassured her daughter that Auntie would soon be fine, but was worried that once again her impulsive sister had created an impossible situation.

The drama was community news, and there was no way to prevent a scathing and sarcastic report from appearing in the local paper.

Pincher Creek Echo, May 17th, 1929
Twin Butte Woman Spent Four Days on Mountains
Claims to have been chased by a bear

Following what may be termed an unsettled life, Mrs. Marshall, formerly Miss Eckland, returned to the home of her brother Alvin in Twin Butte recently.

Miss Eckland was known as a cowgirl rider at the Pincher Creek stampedes of several years ago. She was formerly married to R.

Marshall and finally left and went to the States where after obtaining a divorce, it is stated she again married but with no happier result because this marriage also terminated in divorce. Returning, she and her first husband were again married and again trouble arose and Mrs. Marshall decided to reside at her brother's home.

Trouble again ensued, the brother laying a complaint — his sister having drawn a gun on him. Mrs. Marshall was summoned by Const. Cawsey to appear for the preliminary hearing. That she apparently promised to do, but only after due persuasion, but when the case was called the defendant did not appear. The usual procedure in such a case was followed and it was found that the defendant had gone into the mountains.

A search party was organized by Const. Cawsey and after Mrs. Marshall had been gone four days she was found by Eddy McCarthy in a very weakened condition, having in some way sustained a nasty gash across one of her wrists. She was conveyed to safety.

Mrs. Marshall's story of her disappearance is that she went up into the mountains to hide

> *some papers before coming to town — was chased by a bear and fell over a cutbank.*[8]

Feeling guilty and embarrassed because he thought he had driven his sister to this extreme decision, Alvin withdrew the charges. He was ashamed of Bertha's behaviour and wanted no more publicity. Roy tried to get her to talk to him, to suggest that they try again; however Lala was the only one she would talk to. Bertha was still furious with Alvin. She could not forgive Roy and insisted that he would never see this baby. As her strength returned, she began to formulate her next reckless plan.

CHAPTER SIXTEEN:
"This is the truth, is it not?"

For five weeks Lala watched over her sister and helped her heal. By the end of June, Bertha was feeling stronger. She had spent time thinking about her situation. She had read the Pincher Creek paper and knew that her reputation in the community had become even more scandalous. She realized that she had caused her family real grief and embarrassment. She knew she was a burden to Lala and Jack (his health was still a worry) and she knew that Lala needed her energy to look after her husband and two little girls. A plan began to develop. She would go back to California and Hector would help her start again. She would have this baby far from Alberta.

Over the weeks, Lala and Bertha talked about the future. Lala as always was practical and steady, and discouraged the reckless plans that Bertha started describing. "No, Bertha. There will be consequences," she repeated over and over. Early one day at the beginning of July, Lala was only a bit surprised to find that Bertha was gone.

Bertha had ridden to Pincher Creek and at midnight boarded the train to Calgary. Arriving early in the morning, she spent the day getting ready for her trip to the coast, getting cleaned up, doing a bit of shopping and taking in a movie. She caught the afternoon train to Banff where she stayed for the night. That evening she wrote a short note to Lala with instructions for collecting various personal items and asking her to look after her mail. And she apologized for taking the stockings that Lala had planned to wear to the Spread Eagle picnic. They were probably the only pair of stockings that Lala owned, and Bertha had thoughtlessly taken them. To make up for it she had mailed two pairs of stockings from Calgary. In Banff Bertha also sent a night letter to Hector, asking him to meet her in Vancouver. In the morning she boarded the train and let herself relax and enjoy the trip through the Rockies and on to the coast.

Hector was at the station. Together they went from Vancouver to Victoria for a few days' "holiday". Then they boarded the Pacific Steamship ferry to San Francisco. It was a grand trip and helped Bertha forget all that she had been through in the past terrible months. She was out of touch with Lala for several weeks. She insisted that no one in Twin Butte be told where she was. Once again she was Marge, building yet another new life, buying new clothes, going to shows and enjoying all the pretty things available to her once again. Hector helped her find a place, and although he was busy with his business, he spent as much time with her as he could.

Then the devastating letter from Lala arrived, telling her of Ingra's death on July 12th and describing how she had taken her own life. By the time Bertha got the news at the end of the month, Lala had already made the painful journey to Portland to bury their sister and had returned to Alberta.

Bertha was too late to be of any help. Her guilt was immense. Her grief forced her to withdraw from everyone and she refused to come out of her room for days. She was sure she could have done something to prevent this tragedy if only she had stopped to see Ingra on her way to San Francisco. She had been so close only days before Ingra made her final decision. Instead, thinking only of her own problems, Bertha had taken a relaxing and expensive boat trip to California.

The last time she had seen Ingra had been two years earlier, when the sisters were all together in Twin Butte. They had not said goodbye because of one more disagreement between the sisters, and now Bertha realized that she would never be able to say goodbye to her vulnerable younger sister. She wrote to Lala of her shock and sorrow, but in the same letter included a request for Lala to write to Hector something that he would believe, as again Bertha had told him a story that was only partially accurate:

> *Write something like this to Heck - Since you do not believe some things, here is a little statement of facts. This Margy person went on a hike in the mounts on the 10th day of [...] guess it was May and when the men found her after* <u>*two nights and three days*</u> *in a snow storm she came out looking terrible and with a gash on her wrist evidently done by herself as she was absolutely alone. I sent for the Dr. and took care of her for days until she returned to her own little home which was a few weeks before she left for the US.*
>
> *This is the truth is it not? And that will help me muchly. Someday I will help you.*
>
> *"B"*

Slowly Bertha worked through her grief. Perhaps to take her mind off of her loss and to fill her time, she started to work a few days at a doctor's office. She also registered in a cosmetology course specializing in scalp and facial treatments. Needing a reference, she wrote to Captain Harrison at the Prince of Wales Hotel in Waterton, and was thrilled with his letter describing her as "honest, straightforward and pleasing".

Lala received another very long rambling letter from Bertha in August. It was filled with grief and regret, with gratitude to Lala for saving her life, with worry about Lala's health, and awareness of the newest scandal that the family must be facing as news of Ingra's suicide spread. She wanted to know about everything that was happening in Twin Butte, but reminded Lala that no one was to know where she was. She admitted that in a weak moment, after hearing of Ingra's death, she had written to Roy, and she asked Lala to send on any reply he may write. It is a rambling letter revealing a person in a confused state of mind, dealing with grief and loss, guilt and pain.

This is the last letter that exists from Bertha while she was in California. Bertha's second child, a boy, was born near the end of 1929. The family believes that she surrendered him to be raised by a Catholic family in California. Only Bertha knew who had her child and where he was. The decision to give him up was one she would regret more than anything else in her life.

A thorough family search has not revealed this lost cousin. His identity and name are unknown. Did Bertha feel incapable of being a good mother and raising a child alone? Did she fear losing her independence and freedom? Was it another impulsive act? Was she still so angry with Roy that she wanted to make good her threat that he would never see this baby?

The events of the year that followed are unclear. Bertha had run away to California and to Hector, but so much had changed while she'd been gone. The free and open days of the Roaring Twenties had been replaced by the grim poverty of the Great Depression that would dominate the 1930s.

Bertha could not return to her nursing job where she had developed a questionable reputation; in fact, she now faced the threat of being reported for her misdemeanours. Hector had done what he could but was no longer willing or able to protect her. Perhaps he too had finally grown tired of her broken promises and unpredictable behaviour. Parted from her baby boy, unsure of her relationship with Hector, unable to find work, tormented by her losses, and homesick for her family, she could not find peace.

Once again, she chose to go "home". Within the year, Bertha was back in Alberta.

CHAPTER SEVENTEEN:
"His Honour found the accused guilty"

Was it Roy who found the key to rebuilding their relationship and enticed Bertha to return? He had taken out one of the last remaining homestead quarters in 1931: a remote piece of land at the end of Blind Canyon, folded in the wings of Spread Eagle Mountain. This rough mountain quarter had no access road; only a two-mile trail that ran across a gravel plain and then wound up into the canyon. The trail was relatively dry in the summer, but drifted with crusty hard snowbanks throughout the winter and washed out with the melting runoff of spring. With the mountains as the backyard, the sun went down early, even in the summer, and the winter days were dark by midday. The difficult access and rough terrain that made it unfit for agriculture and uncomfortable for living was likely the reason why no one had settled on this land before.

Bertha was now thirty-three years old and she was attracted to a new project. On this remote scrap of land, she could build a hunting lodge and entertain tourists from faraway places. Her vision was grand and unrealistic. A plan took shape in her mind of a spacious log home. She saw a great room with a huge stone fireplace and vaulted ceilings. She wanted several bedrooms. The door would be on the east side, protected from the ever-present west wind. The floors would be hardwood.

The windows and doors would be big enough to showcase Alberta's blue skies and spectacular mountain views.

It was a project that could only be worked on in the summer months, but it gave Bertha purpose. The location for the cabin was established in a small mountain meadow and the footprint was marked. The logs for the building were found in nearby Yarrow Canyon. Roy, Jack Bechtel and Nels cut the trees and skidded them down to the building site where they were peeled and shaped and stored. They set the foundation that fall and waited for spring to come to begin construction. It seemed that Bertha had given up her reckless ways. Lala was there to help as well, but her time was often consumed by taking care of Nona, Inga and their new baby sister, Jacqueline.

But Bertha had not severed all connections with her California son and the ties were intricate and complex. Some American acquaintances had information that linked her to criminal activity in California. They threatened to expose her unless she sent money. They threatened to prevent her from being able to return to the area where her son was living. She recognized the real possibility that she might never see him again. What seemed to be an easy way to get money and satisfy the blackmailers' demands was proposed. Still impulsive and unpredictable, Bertha believed that because she had been able to make her own rules in the past, she could continue to do so without consequences. She agreed to a plot that would prove disastrous.

Waterton Park again became her territory and this time, her target. The village had grown since the early years, but Nels' log cabin still sat in the center of the village and the grand Prince of Wales Hotel still dominated the skyline. Some of the wardens and eccentric old settlers had moved on. There were new faces joining her old friends in the town. Bertha had noticed that the park was still attracting a steady stream of American visitors. They came from Montana in shiny red excursion buses to stay for a night or two at the Prince of Wales Hotel. They picked up souvenirs at the gift shop and they always paid in American dollars. American money would be familiar in the shops, but with every note being the same colour, it could be confusing regarding denominations. Could a five-dollar bill be made to look like a fifty-dollar bill? Could a reasonable facsimile be produced?

Bertha picked a warm day near the end of June. She donned a fashionable costume, complete with hat and gloves, and made her way to the elegant Prince of Wales Hotel. She paused as she entered the grand lobby to gaze out at the wonderful view of the lakes, and to shake her head at the foolish tourists standing outside on the bluff, being blown about by the ever-present winds. Slowly she turned and entered the gift shop, then casually wandered the aisles, showing an interest in a number of items. She chatted with the young sales clerk and selected a couple of small inexpensive souvenirs. Bertha flashed one of her most charming smiles, asked the clerk to wrap up her purchases, and gave her an American fifty-dollar bill for payment.

The young clerk returned the smile and left saying she would be right back. Bertha waited, and then wandered over to look at the selection of British teas, wondering why it was taking so long for the clerk to return with her package and her change. She began to fear that her plan was about to fail.

Feeling that something was not quite right about this bill, the clerk had taken it to the cashier, who in turn took it to the accountant to be examined. It was the accountant, Mr. Heally, who returned with the bill and with questions for the customer. Bertha reacted with shock and denied any knowledge that the bill could be counterfeit. She insisted that it had been given to her while shopping nearby in Cardston. And then abruptly, she decided that she no longer wanted any souvenirs and turned to leave. Bertha tried to make a hasty retreat.

Mr. Heally didn't stop Bertha, but he also didn't believe her. He had already made a call to the RCMP station and before Bertha could leave the hotel, Corporal Ford intercepted her and insisted she accompany him to the police station. It was a non-negotiable request.

Macleod Gazette
Macleod, Alberta, Thursday July 14th, 1932

Bertha Marshall of Twin Butte appeared in court on Monday, where she elected for a speedy trial on two charges, viz., having in her possession a forged bank note of a fifty dollar bill, knowing it to be forged, and, killing a lamb with intent to steal the carcass thereof. She was released on bail of $7000. The date of hearing has been arranged for August 1st. J. D. Matheson, K. C. appeared for the Crown, and F. O. McKenna is representing the accused.

Judge J. A. MacDonald held chambers here on Monday, Jul 11. The next chambers will be held on August 1st, after the vacation.[9]

These facts were presented in the local newspapers and word travelled quickly among the local gossips. Everyone had a comment or an explanation for Bertha Marshall being in jail as she awaited the judge's arrival in Fort Macleod to hear the case. The Ekelund family members attempted to avoid their neighbours, but were questioned everywhere they went. All they could answer was that Bertha was just "being Bertha".

Lala and Jack arranged for a lawyer and started the process of raising bail. Bertha was released to them and permitted to return to Twin Butte with instructions to stay in the area. They would be required to wait a long two weeks before the judge could hear her case on August 3rd. Bertha had no intention of going to jail. Despite the fact that Lala and Jack would likely lose everything if she jumped bail, she planned her escape: first into British Columbia and, from there, back into the States one more time.

She waited for a clear night with a full moon. This time she donned the costume of a man, complete with broad felt hat under which she tucked her hair. She added a scarf at her neck to hide most of her face. She packed a few important items in her saddle bag, climbed up on her horse and headed for the old trails, first travelled by her First Nations friends, to cross from the Waterton canyons west into British Columbia. They were trails she had travelled many times before. Unfortunately, the local police knew her reputation and her record. They were watching the trails.

Bertha was intercepted by the RCMP in a lonely mountain meadow. Surrounded, she surrendered and was escorted first to Pincher Creek and then to Lethbridge to await her trial.

The trial commenced on August 3rd in Fort Macleod. The Crown summoned seven reliable witnesses to testify. The

Defense had no witnesses to call, opting instead to point out that although the accused had had the note in her possession, she was unaware that it was not legal tender, and that her actions were an innocent mistake. But this time Bertha's actions would catch up with her, and her confident observation that "I have done worse things [...] and got away with it" did not prove to be true in this case.

She had a reputation and a record of attempted escapes. The judge did not accept the defense of innocence and found her guilty. He gave her an unusually harsh sentence: one year in jail. Her punishment was severe, but perhaps surprisingly, no extra time was added for the lamb she was accused of stealing.

Has Forged Bill, Is Given Year
Macleod, Alberta August 3rd, 1932
Yarrow Woman is Found Guilty at Court Sittings in Macleod

> *Sittings of the District Court of the judicial district of Macleod were held in the Court House at Macleod on Monday with His Honour Judge J. M. MacDonald on the bench. There was only one case on the docket. Mrs. Bertha Marshall of Yarrow was charged with having in her possession and trying to pass a $50 forged bank bill, knowing it to be forged, at the Prince of Wales Hotel on Tuesday, June 28th.*

According to the evidence of witnesses examined for the prosecution, the accused went to the gift shop of the hotel and made certain purchases from Miss Card, the lady attendant in charge of the Gift Shop, and tendered the forged bill in payment. Miss Card took the bill to Miss Allan, the cashier, for change, who at once detected that is was a bogus bill and took it to H. Heally, the accountant, who then went and questioned Mrs. Marshall as to where and from whom she had got the bill. The accused stated that she had got it in a store in Cardston. Mr. Heally at once notified Corpl. Ford of the R.C.M.P., who arrested the accused on her way from the hotel.

Evidence for the Crown was given by Corpl. Ford, Miss Kathleen M. Allan, Miss Card, Mrs. Corpl. Ford, H. Heally, Constable R. J. Blair, Waterton Park R.C.M.P. and Detective Corpl. Causey of Lethbridge.

F. O. McKenna, barrister of Pincher Creek, appearing for the accused, did not call any witnesses, but in his address to the Bench, tried to show that the Crown had not proved its case. His Honour, however, found the accused guilty and sentenced her to serve one year in Fort Saskatchewan jail.

> *Another charge was also laid against the accused Mrs. Marshall: that of stealing and killing a lamb, for the purpose of using the carcass. This charge was dismissed by the judge.*
>
> *J. C. Matheson K.C. appeared for the Crown and F. O. McKenna for the accused.*
>
> *At the close of the cases Judge MacDonald held chambers, when several cases were disposed of.*[10]

Lala and Jack Bechtel remained beside her and did everything they could to help. They faced the ridicule of their neighbours. They mortgaged their ranch to raise the seven-thousand-dollar bail* – a significant amount at any time, but a fortune during the depression. They faced the possibility of losing everything, but they would not let her face this alone. Her older brothers distanced themselves from their delinquent sister. Roy was strangely silent and absent.

So many unanswered questions accompany this behaviour. Why would she risk so much by presenting a forged bill as payment for purchases, knowing that fifty dollars was a significant and therefore suspicious amount of money? Who made this bill? Where did it come from? Was it one-of-a-kind or had

---

* Seven-thousand dollars is reported as the bail amount but seems inappropriately large. It is possible that there was an error in the newspaper article. The trial notes have long since been destroyed.

other similar bills been seen in the area recently, alerting storeowners to be watchful?

If Bertha had accomplices or was coerced into passing this bill, she never revealed who else was involved. She stood alone and took the punishment alone.

A documented crime was committed in the summer of 1932 at the Prince of Wales Hotel. Since then the legend of a strange and colourful local character named Bertha who made her own counterfeit money in her cabin, and who was connected to the mob in the U.S., who wrote fake medical prescriptions for alcohol during Prohibition, and who was a prostitute in the early days of the park, has endured. Articles have appeared in local newspapers and magazines, all with slightly varying details, but all branding her as a notorious criminal.

CHAPTER EIGHTEEN:

Prisoner #1590

Bertha stood shocked as she listened to the judge's sentence. It had taken him only minutes to deliver his verdict, and it was final. She was allowed a moment to say goodbye to Lala and Jack before she was escorted out of the courtroom by the police to be taken back to Lethbridge.

At that time very few women were sentenced to jail; Bertha was about to become a member of an exclusive group. Fort Saskatchewan was the only facility in Alberta to incarcerate women sentenced to a year or more. This was the prison that held those awaiting execution. The only woman to be hanged in Alberta, Florence Picarello, had spent her last days there in 1923. Some people insisted that her ghost still walked the halls.

Bertha asked her guards for more information, and everything she heard made her more apprehensive.

Opened in 1915, Fort Saskatchewan was a large and formidable grey building: four stories tall, square and solid in construction, it was overshadowed by a huge water tower and smaller guard towers. Since the beginning of the Great Depression, the Canadian prison system had become regressive and punitive. Jails were overcrowded and inmates were dealt with harshly. There was a process for granting prisoners time off for good behaviour - prisoners could be granted a "ticket of leave" from Ottawa based on their prison record—but it was ambiguous and subjective.

The rewarding of "remission", or time off for good behaviour, was based on points for industry and conduct. Guards kept daily records of the convicts' ratings and the points were tallied in a monthly ledger. In addition to these points, other factors could be considered in granting a ticket, such as: mental debility; extreme youth or old age; or doubt about the convict's guilt. The "ticket" was granted by the Governor General in Ottawa.

Parole Board of Canada

As if this regime were not enough to break the strongest spirit, the convict's existence was defined and circumscribed by a multitude of rules. When General D. M. Ormond became Superintendent of Penitentiaries in 1932, he introduced a draconian policy of militaristic control. Between 1932 and 1934, the number of regulations increased from 194 to 724. By the end of his regime in 1938, there would be 1,500 regulations, covering every possible aspect of prison life, even dictating how a guard should tie his shoes!

Under these circumstances, it was almost impossible for a prisoner to avoid committing

> some offence. Punishments were severe [...] Abuses —even atrocities — went unchallenged because the penitentiaries were a world apart, a secret kingdom cut off from the rest of the community. The Canadian public was indifferent to the plight of prisoners and quite willing to leave the distasteful chore of dealing with them to the proper authorities.
>
> *(from History of Parole in Canada)*[11]

During the 330-mile, two-day trip north, Bertha could only imagine the horror that awaited her. She would be caged, forced to follow strict rules, shut away from the people and places that nourished her. Again her dark depression shared her journey and grew stronger the closer she got to the prison walls.

Bertha shivered as the car moved through the prison gates and entered the courtyard. Bertha was escorted to an admittance room where she was asked a number of questions. Bertha's answers were recorded as the initial entries in the record for prisoner #1590.[12]

Name	Bertha Marshall
Civil State	Married
Age	33
Weight	138 pounds
Height	5'5"
Occupation	Nursing
Creed	Methodist

Even standing before the Fort Saskatchewan warden and facing immediate incarceration, Bertha twisted the truth.

Next there were the humiliations of a physical examination, the allotment of prison garb, and final processing, before being taken to her cell.

Fort Saskatchewan prison life is described by inmate Patrick Lenithan.[13] He paints a dismal picture. She was taken to a miserable little space with bars to separate her from freedom: a bunk with a straw mattress and a washbasin and toilet bowl in the corner. The mattress was made of canvas filled with a thin layer of straw and rested on iron bars. It was little better than sleeping directly on the hard iron bars themselves.

She was forced to adjust to the prison routines, which didn't change from day to day or week to week. Breakfast consisted of a thick piece of bread and a cup of weak tea. Lunch and supper were consistently a thin vegetable stew with the occasional hint of meat. The only variation came thanks to the Catholic Church, which forbade its members to have meat on Friday. Instead the prisoners were all served beans. The portions were small – inmates were always hungry.

The few female inmates were kept separately from the men and although they had little contact with the male convicts, they knew they were vulnerable in this place of potential violence and abuse.

Every ten days or so, at unexpected times, the guards searched each cell, emptying the straw mattresses and poking into every corner in search of anything suspicious. Visitors were allowed on Saturdays for half an hour but only in the presence of two guards. Bertha had no visitors.

The rules did not allow smoking or talking. In the yards and corridors, men were forced to walk in lockstep, their eyes averted from each other. Prisoners could spend up to seventeen hours a day alone in their cells with nothing to do. On Sunday, the Salvation Army came to conduct a church meeting. Few inmates were interested in sitting and talking with a Salvation Army Officer, but many attended just to be in the presence of other people and to escape momentarily from the loneliness and isolation of their cells.

The Fort Saskatchewan prison was less rigid than prisons in eastern Canada. It operated a large farm. The garden provided potatoes and carrots for the daily stew. The cattle provided milk and beef. A gymnasium offered a means to get some exercise. Some inmates were kept busy or taught a trade in the shops.

Bertha worked on the farm through the fall months. The guards learned that she could sew and was an experienced hairdresser, so they put her to work at these tasks when needed. Women prisoners were also put to work in the kitchen and Bertha spent many hours preparing meals. In order to provide food for the prison population, the kitchen needed commercial-sized equipment and walk-in coolers. She never said much about her hand ... only that one day, as the huge heavy door of the freezer swung closed, her left hand was caught between the door and the frame. Was it an accident? Was the door deliberately pushed? The top part of her third finger was smashed and torn off. This shortened finger would be a constant reminder of her time spent in jail, and she tried to cover it up in her remaining years.

Bertha hated being a prisoner, but she forced herself to follow the rules because she knew it would affect the length of her stay. She knew that three days could be subtracted from her sentence for every month of good behaviour, and so she hoped to be released thirty-six days short of her one-year sentence. She calculated and recalculated her remaining time.

Alone in her cell, Bertha's thoughts would turn to better times and places. She dreamed about the southern Alberta countryside: the majestic mountains to the west and the open prairies to the east. She remembered the overwhelming beauty of the panoramic views from the mountain peaks and the clear creeks that tumble from the canyons. She could almost hear the eagles and owls, the badgers and pack rats. She envied the freedom of the deer and moose, the grizzly bears and wolves that lived in open spaces. She even missed the constant west wind … at least it was free. She thought of Lala and Jack and her three darling nieces, but from there her thoughts would drift to Ingra who was gone and whom she had failed, and to Roy, her lost daughter, and the son she had given away.

The days grew shorter, darker and colder as the year faded from summer to winter. Often she was overcome with loneliness and the deep depression that lurked within - the desperation that had walked with her that night in the snow and wind when she had first tried to end her suffering. Again she wanted to end the pain. She struggled to think of the future and of the promise of freedom next summer.

Prisoners could write one letter a month. Bertha wrote to her family in Twin Butte and her aunts in Utah of her despair and desperation. The family feared that she might not survive the sentence, that she may again try to take her own life. Letters were written on her behalf to politicians in both Edmonton and Ottawa describing her state of mind and begging for an early release.

Her only escape was to dream of the day when she would return to her remote mountain cabin. She dreamed of it as an elegant mountain lodge where she could entertain visitors - hunters and tourists who wanted to experience that beautiful part of the world. This was where she would settle, where she would have protection from gossip and criticism and the judgment of prying neighbours. Here she would create a dwelling that was safe and secure yet permitted her the freedom she so desperately missed. Through the long hours alone in her cell, Bertha went over every possibility of her log cabin, adding details to the plans - doors and big, bright windows on every side to allow the light to come in and the inhabitants to get out, conveniences like running water piped in from the stream and an ice house for cold drinks and ice cream in the summer. These dreams kept her going.

Gradually the days turned into weeks and then months. She began to feel the warmth of the early spring sun and see the light of the longer days. She counted the days until her release and was surprised to be called to the warden's office near the end of March. She was unexpectedly informed that she had been granted an early release. Her good behaviour combined with the letters from her family had convinced the warden.

Her Licence under the Ticket of Leave Act was signed in Ottawa on March 30th, 1933. She had been in the prison for eight months (240 days) and was released 125 days before the end of one full year.

Licence Under the Ticket of Leave Act

His Excellency the Governor General is graciously pleased to grant to Mrs. B. Marshall, #1590, who was convicted of (Unlawful possession of forged Bank Note knowing the same to be forged) at Macleod Alberta by his Honour Judge McDonald on the 1st day of August 1932 and was then and there sentenced to imprisonment in the Fort Saskatchewan Goal for the term of 1 year.

This licence is given subject to the conditions herein and may be revoked for breach of the said conditions whether such breach be followed by conviction or not, or it may be altered or revoked or forfeited or liable to forfeiture for any existing cause on the day when the mentioned sentence would expire if reduced by remission earned at the time of the convict's release which day will be specified by the Warden or their proper officers of the Prison in the Margins opposite hereto. Thus the said sentence will be deemed to have been satisfied and this licence will have no further operation or effect. Given under my hand and seal, at Ottawa, the 30th day of March, 1933.

Thomas Mulvey
Undersecretary of State [14]

She left Fort Saskatchewan on April 2nd and arrived in Pincher Creek on April 4th. She was taken directly to the RCMP Office. Conditions of her early release included reporting in person to the same police station on the fifth day of the month of May, June, July and August. At the end of that time the sentence would be deemed to have been satisfied. If she failed to comply, the licence could be revoked.

Seeing her brother Johnny there to meet her made it finally seem real to Bertha that her time in prison was over. Her journey back to Twin Butte seemed endless, but this time, rather than dreading her arrival, she counted the minutes until she was embraced by her family and surrounded by the wings of Spread Eagle Mountain, free to ride with the wind across the open fields. As they headed south Bertha felt the black cloud that had been her companion for the past year, lift.

The woman who returned from Fort Saskatchewan was a more subdued, respectful and careful Bertha.

Bertha Marshall, circa 1935

CHAPTER NINETEEN:

"Bear Paw Cabin"

Eight months of confinement was now over. And freedom felt good!

As she headed south toward her beloved mountains, Bertha again thought about the log cabin that she and Roy had begun building. She hoped that by finishing her own log house she could erase her sense of homelessness. This home had been put on hold when she was sent to jail. Now she could finish the project. She had just turned thirty-five.

Roy too had waited for Bertha's return before continuing with the build. He realized that the time in prison had been a time of torment for Bertha, and was prepared to provide the support and companionship that he could. The unbreakable bond between them, although strained was still intact.

The logs were cured and waiting when Bertha finally arrived at the cabin site. The footprint had been established in an open meadow with a spring running from the adjacent hillside. The plans were finalized. A small icehouse was built beside the spring and a canvas roof and tent were added to provide a tiny home for Roy and Bertha to live in while the bigger house took shape. As each layer of logs was added, Bertha could see her dream becoming a reality. The plan included a great room with a high ceiling, hardwood floors and French doors that opened onto the meadow and the morning sun. There was a kitchen with running water diverted from the spring, a well-lit eating area with windows on three sides, a pantry, two small bedrooms and a loft where visiting nieces could sleep. There were plans for a stone fireplace, and a large stone chimney was constructed using river stones.

Bertha, Roy and Jack Bechtel set to work adding more rounds of logs. And Nels, seeing a way to reconnect with his wayward daughter, offered to help. He had never been much of a support for her as a child, but now he pitched in. As the sturdy log walls of the house grew, the relationship between Bertha and her father matured and they worked together compatibly as adults. He stayed and worked with them, his talents as a carpenter and woodworker were evident in the craftsmanship of the finished project.

The summer months passed quickly, but Bertha was keenly aware of the calendar dates. On the fifth day of each month she presented herself at the Pincher Creek RCMP station as required. Her behaviour and attitude were impeccable.

All too soon the days began to get shorter and the temperatures began to drop. Work on the cabin had to stop and wait for the spring thaw. They secured their project for the winter and turned their attention to getting through the next six months.

Bertha needed money and found a legitimate way to earn it. She opened a beauty parlour in Pincher Creek: *Beauty Villa*. Business was slow at first, but soon word spread that Bertha was good at what she did. Her clients appreciated her skill, her sense of fashion and her sense of humour. Some asked about the disfigured finger and Bertha was quick with a creative story to explain the "accident". She did not share the pain it caused her as a constant reminder of the blackest winter of her life. Bertha was a good businesswoman, and the shop ran smoothly. Only one thing was really irritating to her, and Bertha knew how to deal with that.

The man next door had an obnoxious rooster that didn't follow the rising and setting of the sun, but rather crowed continuously. Bertha's solution was to get rid of it. She baited and caught the rooster, then killed, plucked and cooked him for dinner. Her neighbour would ask, "Have you seen my rooster? Whatever could have happened?" and Bertha would innocently share his bewilderment. Only Lala was told that the rooster made a tasty meal.

Through the winter Bertha planned, as she cut and styled her clients' hair, and a new and grand idea began to take shape. The past year, although very difficult, had not extinguished her spark for spontaneity.

Local rodeos were welcome distractions in the summer months. The winter of 1933–1934 had been cold and dreary and the spring was wet and slow to arrive. Everyone was looking for a diversion. The idea of a Spread Eagle Stampede became the topic of discussion. Roy could gather the best broncs available and invite confident cowboys and cowgirls to try to ride them. Bertha knew she could make this stampede a memorable one.

The Marshalls spread the news through the community that a famous guest, a woman bronc rider named "Lena La Rue", was coming. And the rumour was credible as the Marshalls had connections. After all, they had worked for Guy Weadick and Flores LaDue. Everyone assumed that the famous bronc rider must be a friend of theirs.

The day of the Stampede was sunny and bright. A boisterous crowd gathered on the large open meadow not far from where Bertha and Roy were building their cabin. Community members came from all directions, curious about this promised celebrity but also eager to prove who owned the fastest horses for the upcoming races. Spirited conversation filled the air. The men discussed crops and weather, cattle, horses and hunting. The women considered how the children were growing, how people were faring, and how to get better results in their gardens. Old friends were reacquainted, good horses were discussed, and a few bets were placed. No one noticed when Lala and Bertha disappeared. One o'clock came and went. People started getting restless, ready to start the events. By two o'clock they were really impatient. But the exhibition rider who was supposed to start the stampede had not yet arrived. The crowd waited eagerly.

And then they saw her: a tall, elegant woman stood at the edge of the field. Golden ringlets could be seen falling over her shoulders from under her broad brimmed felt hat. She wore a colourful shirt with blue sequins that sparkled in the sun, a handsome leather skirt and tall boots. Lena La Rue walked into the center of the meadow to the cheers and whistles of the crowd. She smiled and waved her hand gracefully. Roy led her to the horse she was to ride – Meadowlark – a familiar bronc at the local stampedes.

Meadowlark was gentle enough for a child to ride, if they avoided a stampede infield, but very few could stay on once the flank strap was pulled. Meadowlark was snubbed up to another horse and Lena La Rue stepped aboard. Meadowlark ducked her head and started to buck. The crowd cheered at every twist and leap that the little bronc made, but Lena La Rue stayed with her and had no trouble making the ride. As she stepped off the horse, the crowd gathered closer. Everyone wanted to talk to this celebrity, but Lena had another rodeo to attend and was quick to disappear into the crowd.

Bertha, Roy, Lala and Jack struggled to keep their reactions in check. They were laughing because Bertha's disguise of her younger brother Johnny had worked. She had tapped into her many talents to create this make-believe celebrity. Weeks had been spent secretly sewing the colourful costume. Hours had been put into creating and styling the wig. She had carefully applied makeup to the face of her younger brother and transformed him into the elegant lady bronc rider. The local paper reported the ride and the events that followed. People in the community remembered the famous celebrity for years to come.

That afternoon continued with a variety of events: the stake race, the five-eighths-mile open, the Spread Eagle Handicap (with Roy Marshall in second place), the Shetland Pony race (with Inga Bechtel in second place), the squaw race, the half-mile open, the Indian race, the school pony race (with Nona Bechtel in second place), the bucking horse open, the bucking horse local, and calf roping. And the "Best Bucking Horse" was Old Buck, owned by Roy Marshall.

And when the dust settled over the rodeo field, the crowd moved to the wooden dance floor that had been prepared just for the evening. Even a piano had been brought in. Horses were unsaddled and tied in the bushes near the creek. Cars were moved to form a circle around the wooden platform and the seats pulled out to provide benches.

The sun started its descent in the west behind the few clouds that had gathered. A slight breeze cooled the sweaty horses and everyone savoured the cold mountain water they could drink from the nearby stream. Picnic dinners were brought out and eagerly consumed as everyone talked about the highlights of the day. When the piano player and local musicians tuned up and began to play, the couples took to the floor. It was old-fashioned country music with two-steps and waltzes, the butterfly and the schottische. Adults and children of all ages joined the fun and the wooden floor creaked in time with the music. As dusk turned to dark, car headlights were turned on, illuminating the dancers long into the night. Gradually and reluctantly people gathered their belongings, their sleepy children, and their tethered horses, and headed home. There would be only one Spread Eagle Stampede, and it had been a grand event. Dances continued through that summer on the wooden dance floor under the stars, though none was ever quite as good as that first outdoor celebration.

With a successful stampede behind her, Bertha was anxious to get back to finishing the cabin. Again Roy, Jack, Nels and Bertha tackled the construction. It took three years to complete the cabin. There were some people in the community who called her a convict and ridiculed her, but there were others who came to help and joined her family in the build. Bertha knew she was not just building a home, but rebuilding her family and her friendships.

An outhouse, corrals and a barn were added to complete the property. When it was finished, Bertha settled in like a fox in her den. She called it Bear Paw Cabin, a rather ostentatious name for a small cabin, so everyone else called it The Marshall Place. She furnished it with her own eccentric flair. A leather and oak sofa and chair sat comfortably in the great room. Hides were cured and tanned and placed on the floors. She selected the amber colour Depression glass and set the bowls and plates on a shelf by the dining room table. The morning sun sparkled on the grass in the meadow and, through the windows and doors, on the glass on the shelf. Needing a more elegant atmosphere and to bring music to the canyon, Bertha found a grand piano and called on neighbours with a good team of horses and a sturdy wagon who could haul it up the rough road and help her put it in place. Soon the strains of Bertha playing and singing "My Diane" could be heard in the mountain meadow.

The finished home with the Marshalls and their neighbours

She bought a Victrola phonograph and had it hauled to the cabin as well. Her playing and singing were mediocre, but from the phonograph came the sounds of beautiful music that filled the long, dark nights. When she thought the Victrola would make two nice matching end tables, she impulsively took her handsaw to it. Only a few inches from cutting through the top did she realize that with only two legs on each piece they could never stand that way. The Victrola bears the marks to this day.

Once settled, Bertha found the travel between Pincher Creek and her Twin Butte home too onerous and she closed the beauty shop. The first Christmas after the Marshalls moved in, the whole family was invited to share Christmas dinner. It was a true celebration for Bertha. She was free and surrounded by family once again.

Family Christmas at Bear Paw Cabin, 1933
(Left to right) Inga, Nona, Johnny, Bertha,
Roy, Alvin, Jack, Lala and Jacqueline

Living at the end of Blind Canyon was a refuge for Bertha and it was the most beautiful place on earth on a warm summer day. But warm summer days were not the norm. It could be a comfortable home if enough wood had been cut for heat for the long winter; if hunting and fishing provided enough meat for the table; if trade had been done with neighbours for milk, butter, eggs and vegetables; if the early frost did not kill the few vegetables they could grow in the poor alpine soil; if the berry crop was good so that they could can some fruit for winter ... it was a constant struggle to survive.

Because they were always short of money, Bertha and Roy found creative ways to deal with their problems and pay their bills: hunters needed permits but the Marshalls ignored the rules and hunted as needed. They agreed to watch the sheep that local ranchers put in the mountain canyons for summer grazing, and slowly built a small flock of their own. The sheep would spend the day grazing and in the evening they used their dogs to pen them in the corrals to keep them safe from the bears and wolves that walked the trails.

As fall approached the sheep would be rounded up and returned to their owners. Seldom did the count of the neighbours' sheep at the end of the summer match the count that had been taken into the canyon in the spring. Somehow, there were always some sheep missing (coincidentally, the Marshalls often had lamb or mutton as a staple of their summer diet). Occasionally a small herd found its way to the BC market just before the flocks were returned to their owners. Bertha justified this to herself because most of the sheep belonged to the large Mormon Church ranches, and she was sure they could afford to lose a few sheep. If questioned about the number of lambs in the flock, the Marshalls quickly reminded the ranchers that these canyons were the home of numerous predators - bears, cougars, wolves - and it was inevitable that some lambs would be lost.

Bertha sheared their sheep and carded and spun the wool, which she knitted into heavy sweaters or felted into saddle blankets, or even clothes for her nieces.

She always kept at least one black lamb, claiming that every flock needs a black sheep. Her hands were always busy and visitors would marvel at her ability to knit and talk continuously, never looking at her work and never missing a stitch. She also began to sew with buckskin leather, spreading her sewing machine and materials out in the little breakfast nook in the cabin. She made beautifully crafted items and word spread of her sewing skills and artistic talents. She started to receive orders from all over Alberta - more orders than she could fill. She bought tanned deerskin hides and cut and sewed beautiful custom jackets that were the pride and joy of her lucky customers. Leftover pieces of leather were used to make soft gloves, belts, and elegant vests. Whenever she was with other people, she slipped a lovely handmade glove on to her left hand to cover the disfigured, missing finger.

Bertha, wearing her glove, standing at the door of her home

Roy went to work on local ranches and was often away for weeks at a time. He was a capable hand and usually a dependable worker, but old habits are hard to break, and he often found that his money had been spent before he got home to Bertha. Bertha tried a variety of strategies to get Roy's wages before he lost them. Occasionally she would arrive at the ranch where he was working and demand his pay, sometimes pulling out the little revolver that she still carried, as she "asked" for the money. This put her neighbours in an awkward position. How could they pay her for the work that Roy did? How could they argue with the little revolver? When Roy didn't pay his taxes on the land in Blind Canyon where the cabin stood, the title was transferred to Bertha and she made sure everything was cleared up.

Many times Roy's money was spent on a horse. He would watch for the outlaws, the spoiled horses that no one wanted. He was a horse-trader and an expert horseman. He picked up the horses that no one else could ride and brought them home. He and Bertha worked with the horses and, by the time they rode into Lala's yard, he would claim "Hell, any old cripple woman could ride 'em now".

Five and then ten years slipped by. Bertha and Roy were settled in Bear Paw Cabin. It never became the famous hunting lodge that Bertha had once dreamed of. Few changes were made to the original structure. The big stone chimney was never finished as a fireplace. A squatty wood stove remained their source of heat.

Roy and Bertha

And over the years they fought a nonstop battle with Mother Nature over access to the cabin. Winter was the worst time as the sun set behind the mountain at midday and darkness and cold reigned for five long months. Fierce gusting winds, blizzards and snowstorms created barricades of snow along the rough road. With the arrival of spring the trail was transformed into a tumbling creek with muddy slopes and crusty old snow drifts. Only for a few months in the summer and fall could people feel confident that they could get to the cabin and out again. It was then that the mountain meadows became a carpet of brilliant, brave wild flowers, and the summer sun warmed the open space. Too quickly fall would return, accompanied by the blasting of cold, fierce winds and sliding temperatures. The golden leaves would fall and the animals would begin to look for shelter. And too soon winter would set in again.

Bear Paw Cabin – winter

Although Bertha and Roy seemed to have mellowed in their twenty years together, they still had a tempestuous relationship. If Bertha was in a favourable mood, she called him "Skinny". He knew when she was angry, because then it was "Marshall!" Perhaps it was on a day when she was particularly unhappy with Roy that she pulled out her photo albums and with scissors sliced him out of all of her pictures.

Lala and Jack provided a home that was neutral ground for all of the Ekelunds. The family would gather at the Bechtel's for special occasions. Lala prepared the meals, accepting Bertha's offer to help but never surprised when she arrived with a smile and an excuse. Family Christmases came and went. It became a tradition for Christmas dinner to be prepared at Lala's home and the New Year's feast enjoyed at Bertha's. Bertha made the jellied salads and Lala provided most of the rest of the meal. Bertha enjoyed decorating cakes and would finish the Christmas meal by presenting the family with one of her masterpieces. Still unconventional, she would serve her "juice" (wine made from fermented summer berries) and watch her normally stern Mormon brothers become more relaxed and boisterous as the evening wore on.

Roy and Bertha truly valued the support and friendship that came from Jack and Lala, and felt welcome showing up at their ranch any time. The three nieces, Nona, Inga and Jacqueline, loved the unexpected visits from Auntie. They wondered: Was she on horseback? Would she take them riding? Did she have her car, the Essex coupe with the rumble seat? Would she take them into town, driving in her usual careless way, always a bit faster than was safe? Would she bring them something new? Would she have stories that made their mother blush? When those conversations started the girls would be told to go outside and leave the women to talk. How they longed to know what was being said.

The girls loved their eccentric aunt and were always excited to spend time with her and more than willing to take off on any adventure that was suggested. Lala would often intervene and remind the girls that they had jobs to do and remind Bertha that her girls needed boundaries. Nona seemed too much like her unpredictable and impulsive aunt, and was often told by her mother that she could not follow in those footsteps. Lala worried about her girls whenever they left for an adventure with Bertha and Roy.

Bears, usually grizzlies, were numerous in the area and there were frequent encounters. Often they could watch a grizzly sow and her cubs digging roots from the great room window, or a troublesome old boar on the lookout for an easy meal. Travelling to and from the cabin, they would be watchful for a surprise meeting and more than once they were forced to detour around a potentially dangerous bruin. There was respect for the bears and only when other solutions were impossible did the Marshalls resort to trapping and killing these animals.

Many encounters with bears had a serious tone. But one day Bertha watched a little bear cub climb up a tree and impulsively decided to climb up after it. The baby bear screamed when it saw her coming and Bertha looked down to see the mother bear charging out of the bush. Round and round that tree the mother circled, reaching her big paw up and trying to pull Bertha down. At the same time Bertha's dog nipped at the bear's heels. Bertha knew her only hope was to shake the baby bear down, so she shook that tree with all of her strength until finally the baby toppled down and mother and cub headed off, leaving Bertha safe to climb down. Bertha laughed every time she retold this story, but also had to admit that she had been very scared while sharing that not big enough tree with the bear cub.

Every spring when the snow melted and the brown grass began to show hints of green, the bears would emerge from their winter sleep. They were hungry and cranky, and looking for something to fill their bellies. One year a large boar discovered that lambs made a tasty meal and started hanging around the Marshalls' flock. This was a serious problem for Bertha and Roy; they needed to stop this bear before he took all of their lambs.

The Marshalls decided to set a trap. Bear traps are big and heavy, with a huge jaw that is strong enough to hold large prey. These traps would catch and hold a bear, but would not kill it. The trap was placed along a trail they knew the bear travelled and near a carcass he had been feeding on. It was securely anchored with a strong chain around a stout tree. They baited and waited. The next day they went to check the trap. They invited Nona to come along.

It was a quiet ride up the canyon. They left their horses tied to some willows a safe distance away and carefully walked toward the clearing, knowing that this was the most dangerous moment of all: if the animal was securely caught it would be unable to attack them, but it would still require an accurate shot to kill it; if the animal was only held by a claw, or if the trap had not closed properly, they were walking into a deadly situation. Roy carried his rifle. He had three bullets.

It was obvious that the trap had been sprung. The area around it had been trampled as the animal struggled to get free. Now, looking straight at them was the huge bear: very much alive, and very angry. The brown hulk stood up and the massive head with small, beady eyes, red with fury, turned toward them. As they moved one step closer, he roared and lunged with long and deadly claws reaching for them. The sound, the smell, the fury and the power of that animal were terrifying. It represented all that is primitive and powerful. The chain held the trap for the first lunge and Roy raised his rifle.

Nona and Bertha turned and ran; both headed for the nearest sturdy tree and jumped to grab the first branches they could. Unfortunately they had both selected the same tree and their climb to safety was hindered by competition for the next limb, though accelerated by the adrenalin that fuelled their every movement. Roy readied his rifle. As they scrambled higher, the bear lunged again. The trap held. The chain strained. Roy fired. He missed.

Bertha screamed, "Skinny, he's gonna get you!" Two bullets remained and a charging bear would soon be loose. "Skinny! Get him this time!" Roy fired again and watched the second shot hit its mark. The giant bruin dropped just yards from his feet. Roy kept his rifle ready, his finger on the trigger to take his third shot, and waited. They were not safe yet. He knew of overconfident hunters who, thinking a bear was dead, approached carelessly only to have the animal rise up in a final lunge and make them its victim.

It took several minutes for the trio to catch their breath and confirm that the bear would not move again. Bertha and Nona climbed down, more cooperatively than before, to join Roy beside the magnificent animal. Immediately Bertha wondered what she could do with the hide. Nona wondered how much she should tell her mother.

The bear was skinned, the hide was tanned and made into a beautiful bearskin rug that first graced the floors of

Bear Paw Cabin before it eventually made its way to a San Francisco nightclub.

There were times, when weather permitted, that Lala would permit her girls to ride the twenty minute trail up to the Marshall Cabin where they would be allowed to run free, help out with the sheep, the berry picking, or the wine making. Sometimes they just enjoyed the ride with a hope that they would be allowed a sleepover in the loft. Horses and riding were always a part of the summer. Bertha appreciated her mountain paradise and if one of her nieces was lagging behind or complaining on one of their rides, she would circle back and encourage her to keep up, saying, "Step it up kid, this is what the millionaires pay for".

The Marshalls were generous with their nieces and often had little gifts for them. But the girls had been told by their mother to never accept these gifts. All too often the reins or bridles they were given had been hanging in a neighbour's barn the day before. Bertha would often try to repair relations with neighbours by returning items with comments like "This got into Roy's things by mistake and I'm bringing it back".

The local indigenous people used these same mountain canyons to hunt for game in winter months. They would stop at the Bear Paw Cabin, put up their tents, and camp close by. The Marshalls welcomed these neighbours and shared songs, stories and campfires. Gifts were exchanged and the Marshalls proudly added a native drum to the wall of their cabin.

Over the years the Ekelund siblings had continued to hope that Bertha would develop responsible habits, and were relieved to see their unpredictable sister appear to be settling down. But Lala never stopped worrying about her fun-loving, reckless sister and continued to be Bertha's external conscience, warning as she always did about the consequences of irresponsible behaviour.

Within the community there continued to be endless stories about the Marshalls, and people were not shy about sharing them with criticism and sarcasm; they ridiculed her as a convict and spread rumours and stories about what went on in the cabin at the end of Blind Canyon. Some people used Bertha's record to tarnish the reputation of everyone in the family, something that was always painful for Lala and her girls.

And Bertha was not innocent regarding the community gossip. She had always found men attractive and interesting and encouraged special friendships. She would tease Lala saying, "You know I could have Jack any time I wanted to," and she would justify the occasional illicit relationship with the suggestion that "I'm doing their wives a favour because they always come back satisfied and happy". Few questions were asked about the expensive fur coat that Bertha was wearing soon after she returned from a few days away with a local cattle buyer.

Occasionally news would spread that Bertha had visitors from America. She still maintained her connections with her California friends, entertaining those who chose to come to Alberta to see what kept her in this remote, unsettled place. Lala refused to let her girls go to Auntie's place when these guests were visiting, as she was suspicious and blamed them for Bertha's time in jail. Occasionally Bertha, who could not legally return to the United States, found a way to cross the border and return to California for a chance to see her son. Lala was never told when Bertha planned to disappear. She could be gone for days or even weeks, and returned with evasive answers about her time away.

The Bechtel Family
Inga, Jackie, Lala, Jack holding Sally, Nona, September 1942

The extended Ekelund family continued to grow. One more baby was born to Lala and Jack in October of 1940. This baby was a surprise as Lala was now forty-five years old. They named her Sarah Mae after her great-aunt Sara, who had taken care of the three sisters those many years ago. Sally was not a healthy baby and her parents were often worried about her health. They eventually discovered that their baby couldn't tolerate cow's milk, so the family bought a goat from Bertha and set about milking her daily to feed the new baby.

Bertha, Sally and Roy

Sally too got in on the adventures with Auntie and Uncle Roy. She was about five when she was taken to see another bear killed by the Marshalls. The itchy woolen jodhpurs made by her Auntie Bertha were as unforgettable as the fearsome bear that she was told to stand beside.

Brothers Alvin and Johnny were not in a hurry to get married. It was not until November of 1941 that the youngest brother Johnny, at the age of thirty-seven, married Evelyn Pederson. Remembering Bertha's skill at decorating cakes, they asked Bertha to decorate their wedding cake. She agreed, but she had not changed her irresponsible habits. Just the day before the wedding she contacted Johnny to say that she had changed her mind, and he was reminded that it was still a mistake to count on this older sister.

In February of 1942, older brother Alvin, just shy of his fiftieth birthday, married Vera Johnson. All of the five surviving Ekelund siblings, Alvin, Aron, Lala, Bertha and Johnny were now married and living in the Twin Butte area.

Nels watched each of his children marry and settle in the Alberta foothills. He never lost his wondering ways, but spent more of his time at Alvin's ranch, especially once there was a woman's touch. Nels passed away peacefully on December 29th 1943, at the age of eighty. His children remembered him as a restless wanderer and a dreamer always searching for something more. He was buried in the Raymond Cemetery beside his wife, who had predeceased him by almost forty years.

Nels Ekelund

CHAPTER TWENTY:
"It isn't what we want or like"

More years slipped by and Bertha and Roy slowly became recognized and accepted members of the community. In 1944, the attention of the family turned to Lala. They noticed that she didn't have much appetite and was losing weight. They noticed that she was becoming more impatient and irritable, and that she was never willing to talk about what was bothering her. They knew that she had been experiencing stomach discomfort for some time but had attributed it to stress. Lala stoically continued her day-to-day routines, but although she never complained, they could see the strain on her face.

In the spring of 1945, Lala decided to make a long dreamed of visit to her mother's siblings in Utah: her beloved Aunt Sara, and Aunt Eva and Uncle John. Together with young Jacqueline and Sally, she flew to Richfield. They stayed for several months, revisited familiar places and old friends, and enjoyed a wonderful family reunion. And Lala did her best to hide her discomfort.

However, on her return to Alberta she had to admit that she couldn't tolerate food and suffered constant stomach pain. She was too sick to hide her condition any longer and reluctantly made an appointment with the Pincher Creek doctor. She met with Doctor Brayton who gave her a thorough examination and concluded that she probably had severe ulcers. She was put a on a very bland diet of milk, pudding, white bread and clear jelly for three weeks. This was to be followed by an X-ray in August of 1945. The diet did not improve her condition. The X-ray revealed serious tumours in Lala's stomach and abdomen.

The Bechtel Family:
(Left to right) Nona, Lala, Sally, Jacqueline, Jack, Inga, May 21st, 1944.

In October 1945, Lala was sent to Calgary and scheduled for surgery to remove the tumours. She wasn't looking forward to the operation but wrote to her brother: "It isn't what we like or want – It is what we have to have." This had been Lala's approach to life. Her philosophy reflected her serious and responsible nature and her acceptance of all that she had endured.

The operation was not the cure that everyone had hoped for. Lala had stomach cancer, which had spread and was inoperable. She went home to Twin Butte and the family homestead. Her family gathered around her. Jack needed the help of their girls to care for his wife and their preschool daughter. Nona, now married and with a baby of her own, came and spent as much time as she could. Inga was asked to give up her teaching job in the Cypress Hills and come home to help. Jacqueline, now an adventurous teenager, continued with her days at school but was distracted and feeling lost. Little Sally couldn't understand what was happening to her mother. But Bertha could finally do something to help her sister. She put her nursing skills to work and was there to administer the morphine shots when needed, and prepare easily digestible meals. For hours and days she sat with Lala to help her through her worst times.

Slowly winter turned into spring. Helplessly, the family watched Lala's condition deteriorate. Her strength diminished as the pain intensified. She was admitted to the Pincher Creek Hospital for her final days, and on May 14th, 1946, she lost her battle with cancer. Lala was fifty-two. Bertha stood by the graveside and watched her nieces, who were overcome with grief. She could understand what Sally was going through. Forty-two years ago she, as a child of five, had lost her mother. Now Sally, also only five, was experiencing the same loss. It was a sorrowful repetition of a too familiar family scene.

Jack Bechtel took his family back to their Twin Butte home and insisted that Jacqueline finished her grade nine year at the Spread Eagle School. Inga did not return to teaching. She stayed with her father to help out with her two younger sisters. Jack struggled to find a way to manage without the woman he loved, and in the fall decided to take Sally to Vancouver to meet with his family and get help with the problems he now faced. Inga and Jacqueline were left to keep the ranch going.

When Jack returned he had made the decision to stay in Alberta in the home that he and Lala had built. But over the next two years it became obvious that Sally was not a strong child, and when she developed double pneumonia, Jack knew that he had to move his girl closer to medical treatment and into a warmer home. He moved into Pincher Creek and eventually sold the homestead.

The loss of her older sister left Bertha once again without her external conscience, not to mention her most trusted companion, her most forgiving ally, and her source of strength and stability. Lala had been the one person she could be totally honest with and who would stand by her no matter what she did. All that was left was Bertha's promise to be there to help Jack and his four daughters.

Bertha and Roy were close by at Bear Paw Cabin but not close enough to help out every day. Bertha tried. She did some cooking. She made warm gloves and vests as special gifts. She and Roy still dropped in for surprise visits and unexpected adventures. When Inga married a local rancher, Frank Marr, Bertha sewed a special bridesmaid dress for Jacqueline.

Aunt Sara, in Utah, heard of Lala's death and made a trip to Alberta to visit the family. Of the three little girls she had loved and cared for, only Bertha was present to greet her. It was an emotional reunion as the two women remembered their wonderful two years together and thought about all that could have been. Bertha knew it was impossible, but in her heart, she wanted Aunt Sara to stay.

The next year crawled by. In May, Bertha passed her fifty-third birthday at the cabin. It had been a long and dark winter. She had been having frequent, painful headaches. She sometimes felt confused and forgot where she had put things. She made more mistakes when doing simple tasks. She wondered if the wind and the winters were the source of her problems. As usual, Roy had been working away as a hired hand on the local ranches for most of the winter, and she wondered if she could cope with another winter alone. But, true to the Ekelund way, she shared this with no one.

Aunt Sara beside Alvin Twin Butte, August 1951

Although she loved this cabin that had been her home for twenty years, she felt her old restlessness return. What was keeping her in southern Alberta? Over the years she and Roy had lived apart as much as together. She was alone too much; she had too much time to dream and scheme. Without Lala to talk her through the implications of her decision, she convinced herself that a move was a grand idea. British Columbia looked promising.

Bear Paw Cabin was officially registered in her name. She decided to sell and started looking for a buyer: someone else who saw the beauty of the remote location and the potential of a hunting lodge at the end of Blind Canyon. She found a buyer who would take the cabin as it was - furniture and all. The phonograph would be left behind, waiting for someone else to drop the needle and fill the meadow with music

Bertha signed the deal. It would be an uncomplicated move: she had only to pack some clothes and a few dishes into the 1931 two-door black Ford coupe and drive away. Roy - would he come or stay? Because Bertha now had money and, as usual, his pockets were empty, he agreed to go along.

The day they left, Bertha watched Roy from the window of the cabin, putting a few more things in the car. A parade of memories marched through her mind - so many things to remember, and so many things to try to forget.

"Skinny!" she shouted, "Let's go!" They climbed into the car with plans to stop in Pincher Creek to say goodbye to Jack and Sally and Jackie and then head west one more time. Bertha's head was full of ideas for her next career. She expected to make money buying and selling houses, each time for a tidy profit.

The story of Bertha Marshall and her impact on the history of Waterton Park ended as that coupe headed west to British Columbia. Bertha is remembered by her notorious reputation that presents her, in variations, as a colourful character and a dangerous criminal. Tourists ask about the woman who had a mountain peak, a mountain lake, a lakeshore bay, and a waterfall named after her. They are told tales of daring and deceit that Bertha would have found highly amusing. She did love a good story, and often wondered why it should be limited by the truth.

CHAPTER TWENTY-ONE:
Endings

Initially the move seemed positive and promising. Bertha was optimistic about the change. The couple drove west into British Columbia and stopped at a town near Trail where the lead and zinc mining was booming and real estate was selling fast. The town was Genelle, the post office address China Creek.

Bertha described Genelle as very small, consisting of a coffee bar, a garage, and one very small store. The Marshalls decided to settle there and soon were the owners of a neat three-room house with the modern conveniences of electricity, plumbing and central heat. Once the refrigerator, range, clock, radio and lights were all operating, Bertha wrote that "Roy crawls out and turns the switch to make the fire … housekeeping is nice business without those ashes." She continues, "He is as happy as a school kid and is putting on weight now. He dragged the school marm home with him last night and she looks about fifteen but is married and lives down the road." Some things never change.

New furniture was purchased. Fruit trees were bought and planted and the lot was levelled for a garden that soon included a variety of vegetables, raspberries and strawberries. Bertha's plan was to keep the house until they could realize a two-thousand-dollar increase in value and then sell and move on. She saw herself making money without even needing to work.

Bertha loved the warmer temperatures, the early spring, and the absence of wind. She wrote to Jack and her nieces, "R is happy as a cricket and I am at max for sure. The sun is so nice". Three years passed quickly.

Bertha did miss her family and repeatedly invited them to come out to visit. This only happened twice. Her youngest brother Johnny and his family drove out. Her niece Inga brought her family and her sisters Jacqueline and Sally for a short visit. Bertha wished they lived closer. These two visits were cherished.

The China Creek House: Bertha seated at far left, June 1952

Unfortunately Bertha's confusion and forgetfulness did not improve. Some days were good and she cheerfully worked in her garden. Increasingly, however, there were days when she couldn't focus or remember what she had started, or even where she was. Her moods became more unpredictable. Her behaviour became more erratic. This time, however, the behaviour was not that of an eccentric woman doing just what she wanted, impulsive and unconcerned about the consequences. This time something beyond Bertha's control was taking over her life and her mind.

The frequent and angry disagreements with Roy escalated as both began to doubt the wisdom of this move. Following a now familiar pattern, their relationship reached a breaking point and Roy left, returning to southern Alberta to work on the ranches he knew so well. Always particular about her appearance until then, Bertha lost interest in how she looked; she no longer noticed if her hair was combed, if her dress was clean, if she was wearing shoes or not. Gone was the glove on her left hand. Bertha lost interest in what she ate and simply grazed on what she found, as she couldn't focus on cooking. She put on an unhealthy amount of weight. Always a bit paranoid, she now developed a deep mistrust of institutions. She removed all her money from the bank and claimed to have buried it in cans in the backyard. It was never found.

For a long year Bertha lived alone in a place where she had no real friends, no family support, and no one who understood her moods and erratic behaviour. Bertha had made another poorly considered choice, and another mistake. Four years after she left her beloved Bear Paw Cabin, Bertha was reported by her neighbours to be wandering the streets of town poorly dressed and disoriented. She was alone, and she was very ill.

These neighbours called the police, who followed up with a visit to the house. Bertha had only negative memories of dealing with the police, and when she saw them coming she locked the door and refused to let them in. A social worker was contacted and went out to visit, but again Bertha refused to open the door. Realizing that the situation was serious, the social worker, Ms. Gordon, tried a second time, and was eventually able to convince Bertha that they wanted to give her some help.

Once inside, they found that the house had become unsafe for anyone to live in. The electricity bill had not been paid for months and so the power had been cut off. With no heat in December, the pipes had frozen and burst. There was no food, only a kitchen piled high with dirty dishes, dirty clothes and dirty surfaces. The social workers talked quietly and promised to help. They convinced Bertha to move to a nearby hotel. But it was a short-term solution. Bertha caused problems with her continued unpredictable behaviour, wandering the halls barely clothed at any time of the day or night, unable to explain why she was there or what she was doing. Who was this short, round and unhealthy woman who was no longer able to take care of herself? Where was her family?

The concerned social workers took her to the local doctor but they soon realized that her condition would require a referral to a specialist. They questioned Bertha about her family and with kindness and patience got her to share stories of her brother Alvin. When they contacted him they were informed that Bertha had a husband who should be responsible for her. Roy was located and was asked to come and deal with his wife. He did come and he did meet with a social worker in Trail. He did recognize the seriousness of Bertha's condition and followed the local doctors' orders when they arranged for her to be seen by a brain specialist in Vancouver.

On January 31st, 1956, Roy picked up his wife and they drove to the Vancouver General Hospital. He took her to the door. She had one small cardboard suitcase and was wearing her only remaining valuable possession, the expensive fur coat. Roy walked away. It was their final parting.

Bertha walked alone toward the hospital reception. She was disoriented and confused. When questioned, she was able only to give her name and ask for help to ease the terrible headaches. She showed them the referral from the doctor in Trail and was admitted. Bertha underwent surgery for a brain tumour but total removal was not possible and regrowth was expected. Bertha was left with a long, ugly scar snaking across her forehead, and an uncertain future.

With no family to take her home and unable to care for herself, Bertha was transferred to the Provincial Mental Hospital, Essondale, located in Coquitlam BC on February 20th, 1956. Her mental diagnosis was listed as Chronic Brain Syndrome Associated with Brain Tumour.[15] Her prognosis was described as poor: her memory affected, her eyesight deteriorating, her understanding diminished.

Back in Alberta, family members were informed of her admission to Essondale. Her nieces, Nona, Inga and Jaqueline remembered their fun-loving and adventurous aunt and wrote worried letters asking about her condition and recovery. One of her oldest brother June's sons, Junis Jr., who was now living nearby, visited his aunt and shared his observations. It was clear that recovery from the surgery was not possible and that her condition would not improve. Bertha could never leave this hospital and live independently.

Bertha Marshall, patient #38,987, remained at Essondale for six years. She was sometimes argumentative, sometimes friendly, sometimes delusional and always restless. Her independent spirit would surface and she would ask for a horse to be brought to her window so she could ride away. Her anger at Roy remained and she insisted that her fur coat be put in storage and kept out of the hands of Roy Marshall.

Bertha Marguerite Marshall died on March 9th, 1962, at the age of sixty-three. She was buried on the hospital grounds and, although notified, no one from her family attended the service.

Bertha's small gravestone in Essondale Cemetery, BC

But Bertha's spirit does not rest where her body lies. Bertha's restless soul flies free, seeks adventure, breaks the rules and enjoys unbounded freedom. Perhaps her spirit was whispering in the ear of her great-niece Dana when she wrote this song almost fifty years later:

Forest Floors and Timber Trails

They never understood that child
She was always runnin' wild
Though the neighbours talked and the preacher frowned
They couldn't keep her spirit down.
Her mama shook her head and grinned (and said)
"I believe I've given birth to the wind."
Little girl in her nightgown, dancing in the rain
Her head thrown back, she smiled and sang:

> *"Give me forest floors and timber trails*
> *And a horse whose footing never fails.*
> *Give me open spaces, the will to wander*
> *and a lot of room to grow*
> *Give me mountain meadows and starry skies*
> *and the wind whispering through the pines,*
> *If you trust in me and set me free*
> *I'll always come back home."*

He took her hand and changed her name
She does her duty and plays the game
But he knows that she don't belong to him
She gave her heart to the wild, west wind.
And when she's tired of the race

And longs to feel the sun on her face
She rides for the mountains, wants her head in the clouds
And when she reaches the summit she sings out loud ...
When her sunset comes and she knows it's time
She'll lift her eyes and gaze at the sky,
"Well I may be weary and I may be old
But I'm not ready for no streets of gold,"

> *"Just give me forest floors and timber trails*
> *and a horse whose footing never fails.*
> *Give me open spaces, the will to wander*
> *and a lot of room to grow*
> *Give me mountain meadows and starry skies*
> *and the wind whispering through the pines,*
> *If you trust in me and set me free*
> *I'll always come back home."*

Dana Connelly

ACKNOWLEDGMENTS

This book has been years in the making and would not have been possible without the support and encouragement of Jack and Lala's daughters, Nona, Jacqueline and Sally. My mother, Inga, the fourth of the Bechtel sisters, passed away long before I started this project and sadly, I missed the opportunity to add her stories and memories. My aunts, joined by Johnny's daughter Muriel, all Bertha's nieces, shared their memories and stories with honesty and humour. They knew and loved Bertha. It was Sally Connelly (née Bechtel) who collected and preserved the letters written to her mother Lala, as well as the family photographs and the relevant newspaper clippings. Muriel Eklund collected and shared her father John's stories and photos as well as the medical records from Essondale Hospital. I treasure the hours spent with these women - the laughter and the tears. They are true storytellers who have given me great insight into our family.

I also must thank the members of my writing group who always gently pushed me to complete one more chapter and supported my efforts to bring Bertha to life. Without this group, the book would never have been finished. Thank you to the Wonderful Women of Words: Cathy, Gail, Liping, Janice, Faye and Sandra.

And finally, my thanks go to my husband Alan, my daughter Nicole and my friend Denise for their ongoing patience and willingness to review this manuscript again and again.

NOTES

1. Alberta Genealogical Society, "Alberta Genealogical Society Index to Alberta Homestead Records 1870-1930", The Homestead Records, last modified November 14, 2012, http://www.abgensoc.ca/homestead/index.htm

2. Pincher Creek Historical Society, *Prairie Grass to Mountain Pass: History of the Pioneers of Pincher Creek and District* (Pincher Creek, Alberta: Pincher Creek Historical Society, 1974), 742.

3. Frank Goble, "Waterton Hospitality: Kilmorey, Wing Chow and Bertha," Lethbridge Herald, February 24, 1989.

4. I. S. MacLaren, *Mapper of Mountains: M.P Bridgland in the Canadian Rockies, 1902-1930* (Edmonton: University of Alberta Press, 2005), 84.

5. Public School Leaving Diploma and Marriage Certificate of Roy Ross Marshall and Breta Margrate Ekelund, Private Collection.

6. "From Cheyenne to Pendleton: the Rise and Fall of the Rodeo Cowgirl", produced by Steve Wursta, (Bend, OR: Arctic Circle Productions, 2010), DVD.

7. Photograph, Portland Telegram, August 12, 1920.

8. "Twin Butte Woman Spent Four Days on Mountains," Pincher Creek Echo, May 17, 1929.

9. Macleod Gazette, July 14, 1932.

10. "Has Forged Bill, Is Given Year," MacLeod Gazette, July 14, 1932.

11. Government of Canada: Parole Board of Canada, "History of Parole in Canada," Marking Time, last modified October 6, 2016, https://www.canada.ca/en/parole-board/corporate/history-of-parole-in-canada.html.

12. "Bertha Marshall, Prisoner 1590", *List of Prisoners Fort Saskatchewan 1933*, 29, Private Collection.

13. Patrick Lenithan, "The Fort Saskatchewan Jail and Victory in Canada," in *Patrick Lenithan: From Irish Rebel to Founder of Canadian Public Sector Unionism*, edited by Gilbert Levine, Publications of The Canadian Committee on Labour History from 1993 – 2010, (Athabasca, Canada: Athabasca University Press, 1998), 64-65.

14. Government of Canada, License Under the Ticket of Leave Act (Ottawa: 1933), Private Collection.

15. Essondale Hospital Records for Bertha Marshall, Private Collection

BIBLIOGRAPHY

Alberta Genealogical Society, "Alberta Genealogical Society Index to Alberta Homestead Records 1870-1930", The Homestead Records, last modified November 14, 2012, http://www.abgensoc.ca/homestead/index.htm

Eklund, Alvin. Diaries. 1919 and 1928. Private Collection

Eklund, John Edward. *My Own Life Story.* Unpublished Manuscript, 1990. Private Collection

Family letters, clippings and photographs, Private Collection.

"From Cheyenne to Pendleton: the Rise and Fall of the Rodeo Cowgirl", produced by Steve Wursta, Bend, OR: Arctic Circle Productions, 2010.

Government of Canada: Parole Board of Canada, "History of Parole in Canada," Marking Time, last modified October 6, 2016, https://www.canada.ca/en/parole-board/corporate/history-of-parole-in-canada.html.

Lenithan, Patrick, "The Fort Saskatchewan Jail and Victory in Canada," in *Patrick Lenithan: From Irish Rebel to Founder of Canadian Public Sector Unionism*, edited by Gilbert Levine, Publications of The Canadian Committee on Labour History from 1993 – 2010, Athabasca, Canada: Athabasca University Press, 1998.

Maclaren, I. S., *Mapper of Mountains: M. P. Bridgland in the Canadian Rockies 1902-1930*, Edmonton, University of Alberta Press, 2005.

Marriage Certificate of Roy Ross Marshall and Breta Margrate Ekelund, Private Collection.

Pincher Creek Historical Society, *Prairie Grass to Mountain Pass: History of the Pioneers of Pincher Creek and District*. Pincher Creek, Alberta: Pincher Creek Historical Society, 1974.

The family surname has two spellings. Nels' name was spelled Eklund when the family left Sweden. However, his tombstone reads Ekelund. In the family, Alvin and John and their descendants use the spelling Eklund. June, Aron, Lala, Ingra, Bertha and their descendants use the spelling Ekelund.

Printed in Canada